2006

Decks
1-2-3®

Meredith®
B O O K S

Decks 1-2-3®
Editor: Larry Johnston
Copy Chief: Terri Fredrickson
Publishing Operations Manager: Karen Schirm
Senior Editor, Asset and Information Manager: Phillip Morgan
Edit and Design Coordinator: Mary Lee Gavin
Editorial and Design Assistant: Renee E. McAtee
Book Production Managers: Pam Kvitne, Marjorie J. Schenkelberg,
    Rick von Holdt, Mark Weaver
Contributing Copy Editor: Don Gulbrandsen
Contributing Proofreaders: Sue Fetters, Cheri Madison,
    Patrick Smythe-Eagle
Indexer: Barbara L. Klein

**Additional Editorial and Design contributions from
    Abramowitz Creative Studios**
Publishing Director/Designer: Tim Abramowitz
Writer: Martin Miller
Graphic Designers: Kelly Bailey, Joel Wires
Photo Research: Deb Abramowitz, Amber Jones
Photography: Image Studios
    Account Executive: Lisa Egan
    Photographers: Bill Rein, John von Dorn
    Assistants: Rob Resnick, Scott Verber
    Technical Advisor: Rick Nadke
Additional Photography: Doug Hetherington
Illustration: Jim Swanson

Meredith® **Books**
Executive Director, Editorial: Gregory H. Kayko
Executive Director, Design: Matt Strelecki
Managing Editor: Amy Tincher-Durik
Executive Editor/Group Manager: Benjamin W. Allen
Senior Associate Design Director: Tom Wegner
Marketing Product Manager: Brent Wiersma

Publisher and Editor in Chief: James D. Blume
Editorial Director: Linda Raglan Cunningham
Executive Director, New Business Development: Todd M. Davis
Director, Sales-Home Depot: Robb Morris
Executive Director, Sales: Ken Zagor
Director, Operations: George A. Susral
Director, Production: Douglas M. Johnston
Director, Marketing: Amy Nichols
Business Director: Jim Leonard

Vice President and General Manager: Douglas J. Guendel

Meredith Publishing Group
President: Jack Griffin
Senior Vice President: Bob Mate

Meredith Corporation
Chairman and Chief Executive Officer: William T. Kerr
President and Chief Operating Officer: Stephen M. Lacy

In Memoriam: E.T. Meredith III (1933-2003)

The Home Depot®
Marketing Manager: Tom Sattler

Note to the Reader: Due to differing conditions, tools, and individual skills, Meredith Corporation and The Home Depot® assume no responsibility for any damages, injuries suffered, or losses incurred as a result of following the information published in this book. Before beginning any project, review the instructions carefully, and if any doubts or questions remain, consult local experts or authorities. Because codes and regulations vary greatly, you always should check with authorities to ensure that your project complies with all applicable local codes and regulations. Always read and observe all of the safety precautions provided by any tool or equipment manufacturer, and follow all accepted safety procedures.

We are dedicated to providing accurate and helpful do-it-yourself information. We welcome your comments about improving this book and ideas for other books we might offer to home improvement enthusiasts.

Contact us by any of these methods:
Leave a voice message at: 800/678-2093
Write to: Meredith Books, Home Depot Books
    1716 Locust St.
    Des Moines, IA 50309–3023
Send e-mail to: hi123@mdp.com.

How to use this book

Building a deck is one of the most popular and satisfying home improvement projects. You can build any deck using only basic construction skills and tools. It will take longer to build a complex elevated or multilevel deck than a simple rectangular one at ground level, but the work and project sequence are essentially the same. This book shows you how to do that work, from planning and designing your deck to adding custom accessories to it.

Chapter 1 helps you decide what kind of deck to build and helps you design it. Study the anatomy of a deck to become familiar with the way decks are built, then look at the photos on pages 9–11 to start getting some ideas for your own deck. The chapter guides you through planning and design steps to create a deck plan that fits your needs and desires, then shows how to draw plans for the project and estimate the materials you'll need.

Chapter 2 discusses the tools and materials you will use to build your deck, including the latest composite and synthetic materials. These are becoming more popular because they reduce future deck maintenance. In addition, this chapter shows some basic—and beyond—building skills that will make the job go more smoothly and result in a

sturdy, durable, and attractive deck. Throughout the book, "Work Smarter" tips show helpful tricks and techniques and "Buyer's Guide" boxes point out tools and materials that will make the project easier.

Construction begins with laying out the deck location in your yard. Chapter 3 shows those steps and the procedures for attaching the support ledger to your house. Subsequent chapters detail steps in digging and pouring footings, constructing deck framing, laying the decking, building stairs and ramps, installing railings, and constructing deck accessories, such as benches and overhead covers.

The chapters are arranged in the order you will follow to build the deck. Read through the construction chapters (3–9) before you start building to get an idea of how the project will progress. Then, as you work, refer to the book to see how steps are performed and what comes next. "Real World" boxes throughout the construction chapters relate problems that deck builders have encountered—they can help you avoid similar setbacks.

Also before you start work, be sure to check with your local building department. You will probably need a building permit for your deck (see page 24). At various stages, a building inspector will need to check your work.

◀ Whether simple or complex, all decks go together the same way. The instructions in this book will show you how to construct any size or shape deck you want.

Decks 1-2-3
Table of contents

How to use this book 3

Chapter 1
DESIGNING AND PLANNING 6

Anatomy of a deck 8
A gallery of deck designs 9
Choosing a site 12
What's the right size? 14
Considering construction 15

Which decking pattern looks best? 19
Computing the span 20
Drawing plans. 22
Building codes 24
Estimating materials 25

Chapter 2
TOOLS AND MATERIALS 26

Lumber choices. 28
Selecting the right boards 30
Synthetic materials 32
Felt, flashing, and footings 37
Selecting fasteners 38
Choosing framing connectors 40
Basic tool kit: hand tools. 41

Basic power tools 43
Measuring, marking, squaring, and plumbing 44
Circular saw 46
Using a compound mitersaw 49
Using a reciprocating saw 50
Setting up the work site 51

Chapter 3
LAYING OUT A DECK 52

Installing a ledger 54
Laying out footings 62

Layout options for small decks. 66
Laying out a freestanding deck 67

Chapter 4
FOOTINGS 68

Digging footings 70
Mixing concrete 74

Pouring footings 76
Pouring concrete pads 82

Chapter 5
FRAMING 86

Setting and cutting posts. 88

Notching a post 90

Building and installing beams 93

Installing joists 98

Blocking the joists 103

Installing joists around obstructions 104

Chapter 6
DECKING   106

Installing decking 108

Installing diagonal decking 115

Installing synthetic decking 116

Alternate fastening systems 121

Chapter 7
BUILDING STAIRS AND RAMPS   124

Making stringers 128

Building stairs with a landing 134

Wrapping stairs around a corner 138

Building an access ramp 139

Chapter 8
RAILINGS   142

Railing tips 144

Installing railings 148

Railings for angled stairs 154

Railing with coated metal balusters 156

Installing a synthetic railing system 159

Chapter 9
BUILDING DECK ACCESSORIES   162

Attaching skirting and fascia 164

Building benches 166

Building a privacy screen 169

Building an overhead structure 170

Cutting a curved deck 173

Low-voltage lighting 174

Installing decking on a slab 175

Building a floating-foundation deck 176

Chapter 10
MAINTENANCE AND REPAIR   178

Applying finish 180

Cleaning a deck 182

Inspecting a deck 183

Repairing a deck 185

Tearing down an old deck 186

Index 188

Designing and planning

f you're new to home improvement projects, you might be surprised to find that planning and designing your deck can take almost as long as—or sometimes longer than—actually building it. That's OK, though, because it gets you off on the right track—looking carefully at all the possibilities and developing a good solid plan that takes into account your family activities and your sense of style. This will result in a deck that gives you years of enjoyment. You can always tell a deck that was poorly planned—no one uses it.

So take the time to design and plan your deck carefully. Consider how you'll use your deck and how it will relate to your home and yard. Do you plan to barbecue on the deck? Would a hot tub be a relaxing addition? Will large groups of people gather on the deck for parties? Do you need space just to get away from it all, a quiet spot for reading? Do you need just one of these areas or all of them on the same deck? What room in the house will open onto it?

Chapter 1 highlights

ANATOMY OF A DECK
Knowing the name of each part and piece that make up a deck will help you talk intelligently to contractors and home center staff.

A GALLERY OF DECK DESIGNS
To get your creative juices flowing, we've included some examples of stylish decks in various landscapes.

CHOOSING A SITE
It's not wise to just build a deck in your yard without some forethought. You need to consider your terrain, as well as where you need shade, privacy, and protection from the elements.

WHAT'S THE RIGHT SIZE?
There's nothing worse than a deck that is too large or too small. Choosing the right size involves making decisions about what kinds of activities you want to take place and making sure you have enough room for all of them.

CONSIDERING CONSTRUCTION
Different styles solve different problems, but each style has peculiarities of construction you may want to consider.

WHICH DECKING PATTERN LOOKS BEST?
You can lay decking in the traditional pattern parallel to the house, but you may want to take a look at the stunning effects of some alternate patterns.

COMPUTING THE SPAN
All lumber is not created equally. Some species are stronger than others—facts you need to know when you choose your material and design the spans of your deck.

DRAWING PLANS
Putting your plans on paper is the only sure way to create a road map for your project—and to get the required approval of the building department.

BUILDING CODES
Building codes are designed to keep construction safe—and this includes construction of your deck. Codes are not arbitrary. They're the law.

ESTIMATING MATERIALS
Before you run to the home center for materials, you'll need to know how much of everything you'll need—not only lumber, but fasteners, concrete, and a variety of other support materials.

Make sure the deck design meets as many of your needs and provides room for as many of your outdoor activities as possible. And if you plan to add elements such as a spa in the future, build the structure now to accommodate those added amenities; this can save cost and effort when you're ready to purchase and install it.

Browse through home improvement, outdoor living, and handyman magazines. Cut out photographs of any idea you like and throw them in a folder. Study neighbors' decks and make notes. Put these notes in the folder too. Don't think too much now about why something appeals to you; just trust your instincts—they will seldom lead you astray in the initial phase of planning a project. Be sure to read through this entire book for design ideas too. Go shopping for material options. When you've gathered all your ideas, spread them on a table and toss out anything that has lost its initial appeal. Then start thinking about how you will use these concepts for your own deck.

Anatomy of a deck

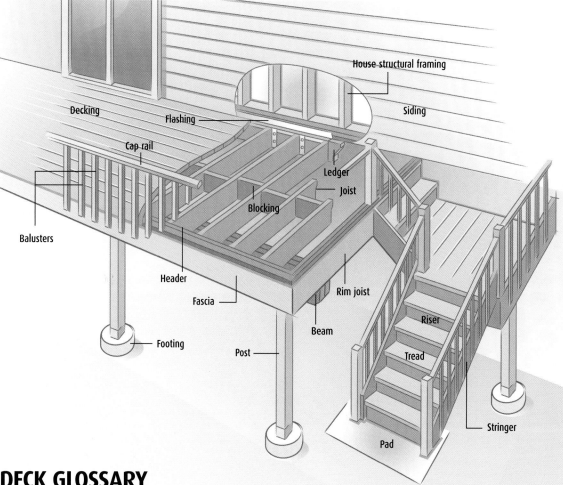

House structural framing

Decking

Flashing

Siding

Cap rail

Ledger

Joist

Blocking

Balusters

Header

Rim joist

Fascia

Riser

Beam

Tread

Footing

Post

Stringer

Pad

DECK GLOSSARY

Baluster: Railing member that divides space between posts.

Beam: Horizontal framing member that supports joists.

Blocking: Short lengths of lumber installed between joists to stabilize them.

Butt joint: Joint between square-cut ends of lumber.

Cap rail: Horizontal railing member laid spanning balusters.

Cure: Process where concrete fully dries and hardens.

Decking: Lumber comprising the floor of the deck.

Fascia: Decorative lengths of lumber, usually cedar or redwood, installed over framing members.

Flashing: Metal used to protect a joint from moisture.

Flush: At the same level as the surrounding or adjoining surface.

Footing: Concrete foundation that supports a structure.

Grade: The surface of the ground.

Header joist: Structural member parallel to the ledger attached across the ends of joists.

Joist: 2× lumber set on edge that supports decking.

Kerf: Space created by the cutting path of a saw blade.

Ledger: Horizontal framing member made from 2× lumber attached to structural framing of the house.

Load: Amount of weight a deck supports. Also known as live load.

Miter: Crosscut a board at an angle other than 90 degrees.

On center: The distance between the center of one piece of lumber to the center of another.

Pad: Concrete slab footing that supports bottom of stairs or heavy accessory such as a spa.

Perimeter joists: Joists that form the outer edges of a deck; rim joists.

Plumb: Exactly vertical. Also, making exactly vertical.

Post: Vertical framing member supporting beams or railing.

Rim joist: 2× lumber set on edge at the outer edge of a deck.

Riser: Vertical section of a step.

Shoulder: Outer edge of a notch or cut.

Square: Surfaces at right angles to each other.

Stringer: 2× lumber installed diagonally that supports steps.

Tack: Temporarily attach a piece of lumber in position.

Through post: Post that passes from a footing through the deck platform to form a support for railing, bench, or arbor.

Toenail: To drive a fastener at an angle.

Tread: Horizontal portion of a step.

A gallery of deck designs

A well-designed deck should be an expression of how you live. Its style, size, and decorative details should match your taste and fit the way you and your family use the deck. Beyond that, your deck should complement its environment—its location in your landscape and the natural elements that surround it. Your deck, therefore, should ideally be somewhat different from any other deck because it is built for you and your lifestyle. With a little imagination, even the simplest of decks or one built from a kit or commercial plans can be a perfect match for your home and family.

▷ A raised deck provides access from the second story of this home along with sheltered space for large gatherings on the lower level. In each area, access to the deck and the activity it's designed for corresponds to that of the adjoining interior room.

▽ A deck can put to use a slope that would otherwise just be a difficult place to mow. Here decks and steps combine with terraced gardens.

△ This low deck provides a transition between the family room and the yard. Though small, it offers space for outdoor dining. Plants help blend the structure into the landscape.

▷ Stairs connect the levels of a deck and function as an important element of style. Here each level is designed as a space with its own identity. Benches provide both seating and storage.

▲ Railings are the primary element for defining the style of a deck. Any pattern or material may be used for a railing as long as it meets local codes (see page 24). Keep in mind that children might easily climb a railing with balusters that aren't vertical.

▲ Wraparound decks connect several interior rooms to the outside and provide more living and entertaining areas. A wraparound is a good choice when you want a deck to provide distinct areas for relaxing, dining, or entertaining.

A pergola provides shade on a sun-washed deck. This one provides a place for hanging baskets of plants; climbing plants can grow on one too.

Extending the upper structure and decking beyond a beam adds architectural interest to the structure and can make posts and beams less visible. Check local codes for restrictions on the amount of permissible overhang.

A freestanding deck can be constructed in almost any shape and offers more opportunity for imaginative design because it doesn't have to conform to the lines of the house. A detached structure can sometimes offer more space than a deck attached to the house.

If your deck site lies in the path of prevailing winds, don't try to block them with a wall or solid fence—the wind will vault over the top. Instead, tame the wind and turn it into a gentle breeze with a lattice screen like this one.

Choosing a site

There's a lot more—or should be—to choosing a location for your deck than merely plunking it down somewhere at the rear of the house. There is no rule that says a deck has to be attached to the house at all. You may find that a detached location, back in the rear part of your yard, provides the perfect spot for a natural getaway. If you plan to put the deck next to the house, take advantage of its exterior walls to get the best fit for your deck design. Also consider the features of your landscape—the slope of the grade, any existing vegetation, views, and climate. All these can affect the design of your deck and where you build it. Don't draw your final plans until you have looked around your yard to see if anything needs changing.

Terrain

The contours of your yard can affect your deck design. If your landscape is fairly level, construction should be uncomplicated. Slopes, even gradual ones, can require grading a level spot at the bottom or building a retaining wall. You could also put a deck at the top of the slope. Posts can reach down the slope and keep the deck level and sturdy, or you can build a multilevel deck to take even better advantage of the site.

Soil

All dirt is not the same; there are countless varieties of soil and they can affect where you put your deck and how you build it. Loose, sandy soil is great for plants, but it may not be good for deck posts. It erodes quickly, and local building codes may require concrete footings in loamy soil. The same goes for silted soil. Water runs off clay soil quickly, and you may have to include some kind of drainage system to divert runoff away from your deck.

▲ When planning your deck site, look for places in your yard where nature provides shade. Trees and shrubs that shade and screen your deck help lower your costs by eliminating the need for building overhead structures or fences.

▲ A deck at the bottom of a slope gains privacy from being hidden by the formation of the landscape. Almost all such locations will require at least a small retaining wall like the one here. Groundcovers can add color but more important, they'll keep the soil in place. Cushions turn the wall into a bench seat.

Sun, shade, wind, and rain

If the sun beats down on your deck mercilessly for most of the afternoon and early evening hours, you may not want to spend much time there. If you put the same deck where trees can shade it from the harsh sunlight, it will be much more enjoyable. Weather patterns can greatly affect the enjoyment of your outdoor space, and taking them into account often makes the difference between a deck that bustles with activity and one that sits empty and idle. If the only place available for your deck suffers from the weather, you can still add some climate control. An umbrella will provide localized shade, or you can build an overhead pergola with open rafters or lattice roofing to shade a large deck. Lattice screens or fence panels will tone down the wind (and add a little privacy too). With a small roofed structure over your dining spot, you can still enjoy the space in inclement weather. A roll-out awning can do the same job, and you can retract it when it's not needed.

▲ **Work with nature, not against it. Trees, large stones, or other permanent landscape features need not push your deck out of an otherwise perfect spot. Build the deck around the obstacle. You'll need a little extra framing to support the decking. If you are building around a tree, check with the garden center to find out how much growth room the tree will need. Be careful to avoid damage to the tree during construction.**

▲ **Make your own shade where nature can't provide it. A stylish table umbrella can make a quick and inexpensive shady spot on a sunny deck. Plan for the future too—plant a small tree now and it will add shade when it grows to its mature size.**

DESIGN TIP

PICTURE THIS . . .

When you're planning the location for your deck, don't leave home without your camera—you'll surprise yourself with the number of hidden (or forgotten) details in your landscape a camera can bring to light. For example, after you've looked at the unadorned sides of your garden shed for a couple of months, it no longer seems unattractive. But put your deck in a spot that brings your focus to the shed and you'll soon be looking for a way to fix the view. In this case a trellis with climbing plants can brighten up the structure (and your outlook). And if the camera reminds you that the neighbors will be able to see the deck and anyone on it, consider a privacy screen.

What's the right size?

When it comes to deciding how large your deck should be, follow the primary guideline: Make your deck large enough to comfortably handle all the activities you want to take place on it.

Start with a sketch of your deck that shows the space needed for each of the activities you expect the deck to accommodate. You'll need enough room for the activity itself, traffic flow through and around the area, and outdoor furniture, which tends to be a little larger than its indoor counterparts.

If you don't think you have enough room in any one area, make that area larger or find ways to make spaces do double duty. If you need space for a private retreat, sometimes you can create just the right feeling in a corner of the deck. Just moving a chair can make a small part of a larger area feel more secluded.

When areas with different functions will be used at the same time, you can separate them visually and physically by using planters, trellises, benches, or a change in decking pattern.

◀ **Large gatherings call for open space and several pieces of furniture. A railing provides safety and adds an architectural element, but it also helps define the space.**

◀ **The right furniture makes best use of deck space. A pair of chaise longues and a small table turn this small deck into a relaxing spot.**

WORK SMARTER

TESTING OUT THE SIZE OF THE SITE

You can't really decide if your proposed deck space will be large enough unless you get out on it. Mark off the area with upside-down spray paint and move in the furniture you'll have on the deck. If you haven't bought the furniture yet, use interior furnishings and add about a foot more space for each item.

Consider the relationship of this deck size with the size of the house. Small decks are usually not out of scale. A large deck, however, can quickly overrun a modest home. Start with a deck that fits the uses you envision and then scale back to fit the limits of your budget and terrain.

Considering construction

All decks are built in pretty much the same order—footings first, followed by posts, beams, joists, decking, and railings. Every deck, however, has specific construction details that will affect cost, material choices (especially lumber size and quantities), and the speed of construction.

The decks featured on the following pages represent the four basic styles most popular with homeowners. As you plan your deck and its location and size, consider also your skill level, how complicated is its construction, and the amount of time you can devote to the project. These factors may not seem to have much to do with your final enjoyment of the space, but they can make all the difference in whether the construction phase is a pleasant, rewarding enterprise or a chore.

One nice thing about building a deck—you can divide the work into phases, and aside from pouring the footings, leave any phase of it unfinished without causing too much family disruption.

Elevated deck

⏱ **TIME TO COMPLETE**

Total approximate time to complete this elevated deck—10 to 12 days, depending on your skill level and the size of the deck.

A raised deck requires sturdy posts and lots of bracing during construction. A raised deck, especially a large one, may need stouter framing—wider and deeper footings, 6× posts instead of 4×, and 2×12 framing lumber. In addition, most of the work is off the ground, which can add to construction time. Scaffolding—an added rental cost—is essential. A raised structure is the only way to provide outdoor access from second-story rooms. And the space beneath virtually doubles the outdoor living area.

▷ **Once you're up there, you may want to leave the entire structure self contained or you may want to provide a way down. It's easy to see how the steps make the deck more attractive and provide quick access to the lower area, increasing versatility.**

Multilevel deck

Total approximate time to complete this multilevel deck—14 to 16 days, depending on your skill level and the size of the deck.

A multilevel deck is actually two or more decks assembled on different levels. This complicates both the layout of the project and its framing. The first visible sign of the different levels shows up when you cut the posts to their heights.

▲ With the posts and beams in place, you can start to see the stairstep pattern this design will finally achieve. The more levels you have and the more differently they are shaped, the more time and attention you'll have to devote to post cutting. The black layer on the beams is a self-sealing membrane that protects the beams from moisture damage.

▲ What adds interest to this design is the interplay of the lines created by the levels themselves, the meandering side railings, the contrast of the metal balusters, and the stairs angled out into the yard. All of these elements keep the structure from feeling like a rectangular outdoor cage.

Ground-level deck

Approximate time to assemble this deck—about 10 days per side.

Ground-level decks are not that much less complicated than other deck styles—they're just closer to the ground. That, however, makes them easier to work on. All things being equal, ground-level decks will tend to be less expensive. You probably won't need 6×6 posts, for example, or at least not as many of them. Footing dimensions may also be smaller, requiring less concrete and reducing costs.

▽ Ground-level decks are easier to build, but that doesn't mean they can't be stylish. Here a diagonal doubled beam has been added to the framing to support the ends of the decking boards for a mitered corner.

▲ Even though this is a low deck, it still requires a railing, partly because it surrounds a pool and partly because local codes require railings even for a ground-hugger like this. Railing codes vary from locality to locality. Check with your building department before you start drawing plans and ordering lumber.

▲ A diagonal beam within the structure of a deck usually requires more complex construction. Notice how the joists proceed across much of the deck set in joist hangers. Those attached to the diagonal beam at the rear of the structure use skewable joist hangers for support (see page 96).

1

DESIGNING AND PLANNING

Freestanding deck

TIME TO COMPLETE

Total approximate time to assemble this freestanding deck—2 to 3 days, depending on your skill level and the size of the deck.

Freestanding decks are fun, but laying them out can be challenging. You don't have the house or any other structure for reference, so the layout phase of this project requires careful attention. Before you set batterboards and mason's lines (pages 62–65), outline the area with upside-down spray paint. Study the marked area from different sections of the yard and from within the area itself to make sure it's positioned properly relative to other elements in the landscape. Use tube forms to level the footings a few inches above ground level.

▶ Internal dimensions and square are easy to check on a low, freestanding structure because access to the various structural elements is easier.

◀ Framing and the remaining construction methods for a freestanding deck are the same as for any other structure. This design, however, is close enough to the ground that the perimeter joists can be set directly on the footings. Posts would be necessary if the deck was higher.

Which decking pattern looks best?

Decking is commonly laid perpendicular to the joists and parallel to the adjoining wall of the house. Aside from the ease of installation, there's a reason for that—parallel decking complements the lines of the house. There are, however, other decking patterns that can make your deck look more interesting. The ones illustrated here are just a few of the options. Changing the pattern of the boards across the surface of the deck also lends you a practical tool for visually separating areas designed for different purposes. No matter what the reason, you'll notice that these alternatives always call for joist layouts different from the usual parallel decking.

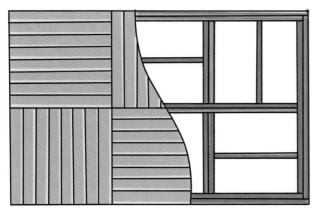

MODULAR
Modular decking is laid in sections, and each section requires joists running in the correct direction. The joists are doubled where the decking boards meet at right angles.

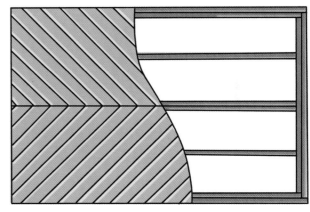

CHEVRON
Although you should space joists 16 inches on center for 2×4, 2×6, or ⁵⁄₄×6 perpendicular decking, you must space them 12 inches apart for ⁵⁄₄ ×6 diagonal decking. Mixing 2×4 with 2×6 decking is another appealing design possibility. Don't use boards wider than 6 inches because they are more likely to cup and split.

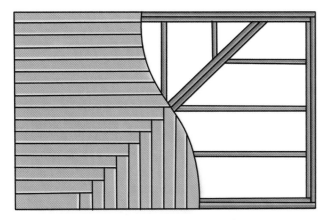

90° HERRINGBONE
The 90-degree herringbone is one of the most interesting decking patterns, but requires a combination of both single and doubled joists to provide support where the ends of the decking meet.

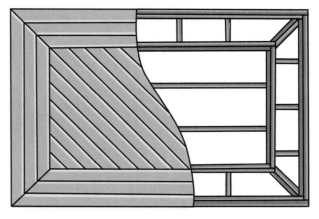

FRAMED DIAGONAL
The framed diagonal provides an interesting visual effect by juxtaposing the two different lines. This pattern can be used to "picture frame" an entire deck surface, or in modular sections to help define different areas of the deck.

Computing the span

When you build your deck, you'll start with the footings and work up to the decking. Designing a deck, however, starts on the deck and works down; you can't just throw in an arbitrary selection of lumber with arbitrary spacing and dimensions. How you build your deck will depend on the size of the deck, the lumber you use, and the distances the various elements have to span.

To get all this to come out right, first choose the decking you want to use and then calculate the length of the joists and beams and the number of footings with the help of these tables.

The illustration at right shows an 8-foot-high,10×18-foot deck with ⁵⁄₄×6 decking of treated Southern pine (group A in wood species chart, right), laid flat. Values in the tables that were used for the example deck are in red type. Use construction-grade lumber or better.

Spans for synthetic decking are different. Follow the manufacturer's recommendations carefully when using these materials.

SAMPLE DECK

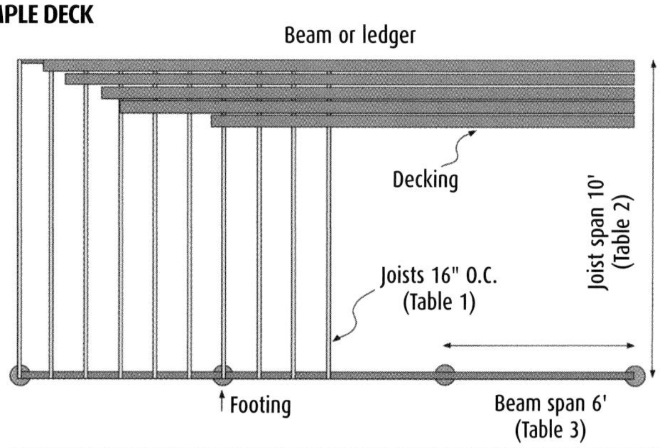

Wood species

A   Douglas fir, larch, and Southern pine
B   Western red cedar, white fir, pines other than Southern and Eastern, and Sitka spruce
C   Northern and Southern white cedar, balsam fir, and redwood

1 Recommended span between joists

Decking	Species	
	A	B/C
1×4 or 1×6 perpendicular to joist	12"	(NR*)
⁵⁄₄×6 perpendicular to joist	16"	16"
⁵⁄₄×6 45-degree angle to joist	16"	12"
2×4 or 2×6 perpendicular to joist	24"	16"
2×4 or 2×6 45-degree angle to joist	16"	16"

*Not recommended

2 Maximum joist spans

Species	Joist Size	Joist Spacing	
		16"	24"
A	2×6	9'9"	7'11"
	2×8	12'10"	10'6"
	2×10	16'5"	13'4"
B	2×6	8'7"	7'0"
	2×8	11'4"	10'6"
	2×10	14'6"	11'10"
C	2×6	7'9"	6'2"
	2×8	10'2"	8'1"
	2×10	13'0"	10'4"

▲ **TABLE 1 shows joist spacing for the kind of decking you are using. For species A ⁵⁄₄×6 decking, the joists should be 16 inches on center.**

⊞ **WORK SMARTER**

BE SURE YOUR STRUCTURE MEETS CODE

Always check with a building inspector about local codes for lumber, spans, joists, beams, and footings before you plan your deck. Information in this book is based on general building code regulations, but local codes always set the final standards.

▲ **TABLE 2 shows how long joists can be between supports. Species A 2×6 joists 16 inches on center (O.C.) can span only 9 feet, 9 inches. But 2×8 joists can span 12 feet, 10 inches. This means you can safely put a beam 10 feet from the ledger, or at the outer edge of the sample deck, if you use 2×8 joists. This will make framing simpler and less expensive. Select the joist size based on deck size and post and beam placement. Larger decks require larger joists but that will reduce the number of posts and footings.**

3 Maximum beam or ledger spans

Spacing Between Beams	Beam Size	Allowable Beam Spans Between Posts Species of Wood (see chart, opposite)		
		A	B	C
48"	4×6	6'0"	5'10"	5'10"
	3×8	8'10"	7'9"	7'6"
	4×8	10'0"	9'0"	8'2"
	3×10	11'0"	10'4"	9'6"
	4×10	12'0"	11'4"	10'6"
	3×12	13'0"	12'0"	11'4"
	4×12	14'0"	13'0"	12'4"
60"	4×6	5'10"	5'8"	5'6"
	3×8	7'6"	7'0"	6'8"
	4×8	9'7"	8'6"	8'0"
	3×10	10'6"	9'8"	9'0"
	4×10	11'4"	10'4"	9'10"
	3×12	12'4"	11'4"	11'4"
	4×12	13'6"	12'6"	12'0"
72"	4×6	5'6"	5'5"	5'2"
	3×8	7'0"	6'6"	6'2"
	4×8	9'0"	8'2"	7'9"
	3×10	10'2"	9'4"	8'9"
	4×10	11'2"	10'2"	9'6"
	3×12	12'0"	11'0"	10'0"
	4×12	13'0"	12'0"	11'6"
84"	4×6	4'0"	4'0"	3'8"
	3×8	6'6"	6'0"	5'10"
	4×8	8'4"	7'10"	7'4"
	3×10	9'8"	9'0"	8'6"
	4×10	11'0"	10'0"	9'2"
	3×12	11'6"	10'6"	10'6"
	4×12	12'6"	11'6"	11'0"
96"	3×8	6'2"	5'10"	5'6"
	4×8	8'0"	7'6"	7'0"
	3×10	9'0"	8'4"	8'0"
	4×10	10'0"	9'4"	8'6"
	3×12	11'6"	10'6"	10'0"
	4×12	12'0"	11'0"	10'6"
108"	4×8	7'0"	6'6"	6'0"
	3×10	8'0"	7'4"	6'10"
	4×10	9'0"	8'4"	7'8"
	3×12	10'0"	9'0"	8'6"
	4×12	10'8"	10'2"	9'6"
120"	4×8	6'0"	5'8"	5'2"
	3×10	7'0"	6'6"	6'0"
	4×10	8'0"	7'4"	6'8"
	3×12	9'0"	8'0"	7'6"
	4×12	10'0"	9'6"	9'0"

◄ **TABLE 3** shows how far apart the posts under the beam need to be. The beam in the sample is 10 feet from the ledger (considered to be another beam, for spacing), so a 3×10 beam with posts placed 6 feet apart will do the job. Posts could be 7 feet apart with species A, but that would make the spacing uneven. Spans can be less than listed.

4 Post sizing

Maximum Load Area Posts Can Carry by Species			Deck Height
A	B	C	6 Feet
144	144	144	4×4
144	144	144	4×6
144	144	144	6×6
A	B	C	8 Feet
144	132	96	4×4
144	144	144	4×6
144	144	144	6×6
A	B	C	10 Feet
108	84	60	4×4
144	132	96	4×6
144	144	144	6×6
A	B	C	12 Feet
36	—	—	4×4
120	84	60	4×6
144	132	132	6×6

▲ **TABLE 4** helps you determine the post size required to support your deck. Knowing the beam spacing (in feet) and post spacing (in feet, both from the previous tables) allows you to determine post sizes. Multiply 10 (beam spacing of 10 feet for the example) times 6 (post spacing of 6 feet) to find the load area, 60. Table 4 shows that for an 8-foot-high deck, any species of the three post sizes shown will hold the load area. Use the 4×4s; they are the least expensive.

If the beams were 12 feet apart set on posts 8 feet apart, the load area in Table 4 would be 96. If you wanted to use 4×4 redwood posts (species group C), you could go up to 8 feet of elevation. But you would need a 4×6 post to go to 10 feet. Decks raised more than 6 feet require additional post bracing regardless of the post size.

The number of posts determines the position and number of footings. Footing size depends on local soil conditions and the depth of the frost line; check with your local building department. (See Chapter 4, beginning on page 68.)

The tables assume a live load on the deck of 60 pounds per square foot. If your building code permits lighter design loads, permissible spans may be longer or dimensions smaller. Check with your local building department or inspector.

Drawing plans

Well-prepared plans will help the deck project go more smoothly, from buying materials to building the stairs and railings. And you will need plans to work with the local building department.

Building a deck in most communities requires a building permit. Before issuing you that permit, the building department will probably want to review your plans. As the job progresses, you will have to deal with a building inspector too (page 24).

The plans you need are a plan view (an overhead view, like the one shown below) and an elevation (a side view, like the one shown on the opposite page). You may also need detailed drawings, which show close-up how some of the elements of the deck are put together, like the railing detail on the opposite page.

Each of these drawings should contain notes that identify the kind of material, the spacing between various members, distances from the ground, and other design information. Make more than one drawing to include all of this information if necessary. The elevation should show footing depth, deck height, and railing spacings. Draw your plans on graph paper using a scale of ¼ inch = 1 foot. Or use a computer-generated plan-drawing system at your local building center if available.

To make the plans most useful, draw every framing piece. That will make it easier in the long run, especially when you estimate how much lumber you need and place your order. You simply count how many of each size board you'll need. (Add about 10-15 percent for waste and mistakes.) You can also use your plans to figure the lengths of decking to buy if the deck is wider than can be spanned with a continuous board.

The ideal plan

At a minimum you need sketches of your deck that will act as your guide and will satisfy the building inspector. The best place to start this process is with a site plan—a bird's-eye view of your property, including the deck. Developing a site plan means going outside—with a clipboard, pencil, and a 100-foot tape measure.

Start with a plot map of your property (you can get one at your municipal clerk's office). The plot map shows your house and all existing permanent features in the yard. Sketch in your proposed deck and measure the distances from it to all the permanent features, such as trees or the garage. Note window and door locations on the side of the house where the deck will be, and indicate their placement with precise dimensions. Then

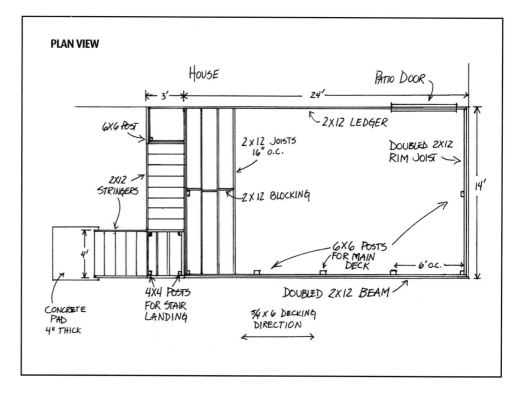

note the things about the landscape you need to consider—things like prevailing winds, angles from which you need privacy, views you'd like to block because they're unattractive. These notes will help you make sure you have everything covered that will make your deck not just a platform, but a pleasant place to be.

Then take your sketch back inside and make a detailed site plan. If a tree is in the way, mark it for removal. If you plan to plant a tree, designate its location on the plan. If a fence needs to go up along your property line, add that in your drawing too. If you're building a freestanding deck at the rear of the yard, draw in the paths you will build to get to and from it. If you need an overhead structure to increase the shade on your deck, include that on the plan view and draw both a separate plan view and elevation of this structure. Once the site plan is done, then draw the plans specific to the deck structure itself.

Waste not

Waste can quickly drive up the cost of a deck. You can reduce waste by designing your deck to take advantage of stock lumber sizes. For example, lumber is sold in even-numbered lengths (8-foot, 10-foot, 12-foot, and so on). If you design your deck so its dimensions correspond to these lengths where possible, you'll reduce cutting and minimize waste. For example, if your plan calls for joists 12 feet 3 inches long, you will have to buy 14-foot boards and waste almost 2 feet for every joist you cut. You can solve the problem by altering the dimensions of your deck slightly so you can use standard 12-foot lumber for your joists.

RAILING DETAIL

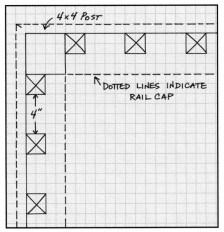

ELEVATION

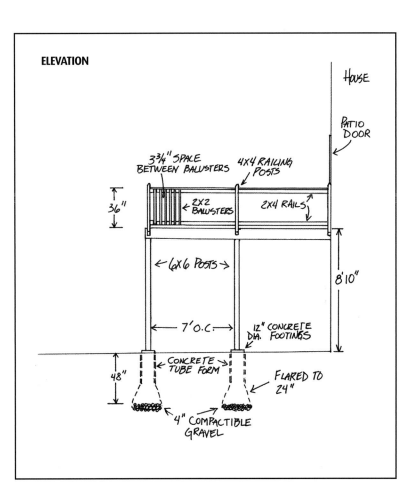

WORK SMARTER

COMPUTER-ASSISTED PLANS

Many large home centers have computerized deck planning programs and offer this service to their customers. Most outlets employ staff who know how to run these programs and they'll be more than happy to assist you. You'll still need to bring a rough drawing with dimensions (height, width, and length) so they have some place to start. If you're computer savvy yourself, you can find similar planning software on the Internet. Most programs produce several drawings—a plan view, an elevation, and a perspective view. Some will produce a three-dimensional view of the deck, including any amenities you want. Many also will produce a list of lumber and materials.

Building codes

Almost all communities have building codes to ensure that materials and methods employed in the construction of major residential structures are safe. A deck is almost always considered a major structure.

Sometimes a homeowner may feel that a code requirement is unnecessary, but most are based on common sense safety. Here are some of the usual requirements governing the construction of decks.

Codes almost always specify maximum spans according to the type of wood used. They are also likely to stipulate that a deck more than 2 feet or two steps above ground have a railing. Codes will dictate how high the railing must be, as well as the baluster orientation and spacing. Small children must not be able to climb the railing or get their heads stuck between balusters. Some codes require separate handrails, not just cap rails, for stairs.

If you anchor the deck to the house with a ledger, codes will state how many fasteners of what type must be used.

Metal flashing of a specific type is also likely to be required. Many codes also demand that posts be held in place by a specific type of post base.

In cold areas many codes require footings that extend below the frost line so that the deck does not raise up in the winter due to frost heave. Other departments may allow a floating deck with shallower footings that move with freeze/thaw cycles. Soil conditions and ground slope may also affect footing requirements.

In addition to building codes, communities, especially large ones, may have zoning ordinances that govern the placement of structures and the uses of property. You may also encounter deed restrictions, which act to limit architectural style, especially in historic sections of the city, and easements, which allow utility companies access to their lines as they cross your property. The building officials will steer you to other departments within local government whose requirements can affect your deck project.

THE BUILDING INSPECTOR
The building inspector usually will inspect your project at several steps in the building process. Find out when these inspections must take place and allow for them in your building schedule. Here the inspector is checking for proper footing depth.

Estimating materials

stimating the amount of material you will need is part art, part science. You may not hit the quantities exactly right, but you can get close with the formulas and methods on this page. It's also wise to check the return policy of your supplier. Make sure you can bring back saleable items for a full refund.

ESTIMATING LUMBER

For a small deck (10×12 feet, for example), determine how much lumber you'll need by using your detailed plans to count all the pieces of each size—12-foot 2×4s, 8-foot 2×6s, and so on—for all framing members, including stairs and railings. Add 10 percent to framing and 15 percent to decking to allow for waste.

Calculate the decking required based on the actual width of the boards you will use, including the gap between boards. The ends of stock decking lengths won't always fall exactly on joists spaced on 16-inch centers. Figure the lengths necessary to fit the joist spacing with minimum waste. (Add an additional 15 percent for diagonal decking.)

For larger decks you can calculate the total square footage of decking you need by multiplying the length of the deck surface times the width. Allow for overhangs. Then buy enough lineal feet of decking to make up the deck area plus the waste allowance. Make actual counts of posts, beams, joists, and other framing members.

ESTIMATING CONCRETE
For Round Footings:

1. Multiply half the hole diameter in inches times itself. (For a 12-inch hole, for example, this would be 6 inches × 6 inches = 36 square inches)

2. Multiply this by 3.14. (36 square inches × 3.14 = 113.04 square inches)

3. Multiply this by the depth of the hole in inches. (113.04 square inches × 48 inches = 5425.9 cubic inches)

4. Divide this by 1728 to find the amount of concrete required in cubic feet (1728 cubic inches = 1 cubic foot). (5425.9 cubic inches ÷ 1728 = 3.14 cubic feet of concrete for one 12-inch-diameter hole that is 48 inches deep)

5. A 60-pound bag of premix concrete will make ½ cubic foot, so divide the total cubic feet for all footings by .5 to find the number of bags (6.28 for the example; mix seven bags). Or tell your concrete supplier how many cubic feet you need for delivery of ready-mixed concrete (see page 75). To convert larger amounts to cubic yards, divide cubic feet by 27.

For Rectangular Pads and Footings:

1. Multiply the length times the width of the area in inches. (Ex.: 36 × 36 = 1296)

2. Multiply this by the depth of the area in inches. (Ex.: 1296 × 4 = 5184)

3. Divide this by 1728 to find the cubic feet of concrete required. (Ex.: 5184 ÷ 1728 = 3 cubic feet of concrete for a 36 × 36-inch pad that is 4 inches thick)

4. See Step 5, above.

ESTIMATING HARDWARE

Count the number of metal connectors and fasteners necessary for the framing (pages 38–40). Estimate 5 pounds of screws (or nails) for every 100 square feet of decking.

COMPUTING STAIR AND RAILING DIMENSIONS

Before you place your material order, determine how much lumber you'll need for stairs and railings. Refer to your drawings to determine the number of posts, balusters, rails, stair treads, and stringers. Because actual on-site dimensions can vary from drawings and estimates, be sure to take actual on-site measurements before constructing stairs or railings.

WORK SMARTER

LENGTH OF LUMBER
Lumber lengths come in even 2-foot intervals. Most stock is slightly longer than stated—a 12-foot board may measure 144¼ inches, for example. If you will cut several lengths from a board, allow for the saw kerf when estimating.

Tools and materials

hoosing materials is a phase of deck building halfway between design and construction. In most cases it's better to choose materials before you draw your final plans—just in case there's something available in your home center you weren't aware of.

Even though you may be anxious to get to the actual building of your deck, it's wise to take your time when choosing materials. If you haven't been to your home center recently, take time to look around at the new products that can make your project easier and better.

While you're at it, this is the time to fill any vacancies in your tool box. You'll want everything on hand when you begin the job. If you're an experienced do-it-yourselfer, you probably have most or all of the tools you need. But if there are tools yet waiting on your shopping list, buy the best you can afford. This applies to everything, from drill bits to circular

Chapter 2 highlights

LUMBER CHOICES
There are several wood species to consider for deck construction. They differ in cost and characteristics.
28

SELECTING THE RIGHT BOARDS
Know what to look for when you go to the lumber aisles to select lumber for your deck.
30

SYNTHETIC MATERIALS
Synthetic materials are becoming more popular. They offer the possibility of a virtually maintenance-free structure.
32

FELT, FLASHING, AND FOOTINGS
These materials are critical to the success of your deck.
37

SELECTING FASTENERS
Choose the right fasteners for the job, so you won't waste time and energy building a structure that won't last.
38

CHOOSING FRAMING CONNECTORS
Framing connectors make a wooden deck stronger. Use them where necessary for a durable deck.
40

BASIC HAND TOOLS
Although power tools have made many tasks easier over the years, there is still a variety of hand tools you can't get along without.
41

BASIC POWER TOOLS
You won't need many power tools to build a deck but the few you use will save you hours of effort.
43

MEASURING, MARKING, SQUARING, PLUMBING
These four skills will ensure a strong, long-lasting deck. They will quickly become second nature as you work.
44

CIRCULAR SAW
This is the tool you'll use more frequently than any other (except maybe your tape measure).
46

USING A COMPOUND MITERSAW
This tool is indispensable for cutting angles. You can rent one if you don't want to buy one.
49

USING A RECIPROCATING SAW
A reciprocating saw is like a giant motorized hacksaw. It's a versatile tool that's perfect for cutting posts.
50

SETTING UP THE WORK SITE
An organized work site speeds the job and reduces frustration. It also helps your project proceed safely.
51

saws. Nothing is worse, wastes more time, and generates more frustration than to stop working on a project to run to the home center for a replacement tool.

When you need a specialized tool for just a short time (for example, a power auger for digging footing holes), reserve it for the day on which you'll be ready to use it. That way, you'll keep your rental costs down. Be sure to check the rental center policy on weekend returns. Some places will charge you for a Sunday use, even if they are not open for you to return it on Sunday.

Lumber choices

Like all material choices, selecting lumber means striking a balance between beauty and budget. This job is made somewhat easier by the fact that aesthetic concerns can take a back seat when choosing structural lumber for posts, beams, and joists.

Here are the major categories of lumber you can consider.

Pressure-treated lumber

Pressure-treated lumber (PT), usually pine or fir, is infused with chemicals that make it rot resistant. The chemicals also give the wood a colored cast, which you can hide with stain or paint. You can leave it untreated to let it weather to a dark gray. Pressure-treated lumber is the least expensive of your lumber choices, but you'll have to choose each board carefully to get stock that is straight and free of loose knots.

Southern yellow pine is a good PT choice. It's strong, hard, and usually not marred with incisions used in the treatment process of other woods. It does have a tendency to warp and splinter, however (as do fir species), but you can control warping with proper storage techniques (see "Storing Lumber," page 31).

Naturally resistant species

Cedar and redwood (plus cypress in the South) are naturally resistant to rot and insects—they do not require pressure treatment. One caveat, however, about these woods—only the heartwood (the darker wood at the center of the tree) is rot resistant. Sapwood (the lighter, cream-colored wood closer to the outside of the tree) is no more rot resistant than a matchstick. Heartwood of these species is becoming extremely scarce and expensive, so most of what you'll find today includes sapwood. You'll have to treat such material with a preservative.

You can seal or stain all these woods to retain their natural appearance. Left untreated, they will weather to various shades of gray.

DECKING LUMBER

Pressure-treated ⁵⁄₄×6   Cedar ⁵⁄₄×6

⊘ SAFETY ALERT

WORKING WITH PRESSURE-TREATED LUMBER

Copper-base compounds have replaced formulations containing arsenic for lumber treatment. Until December 2003, the primary pressure treatment for wood used chromated copper arsenic (CCA) as its preservative. The new alkaline copper quaternary (ACQ) or copper azole treatments are safe for people, animals, and plants when used as recommended. Follow these precautions for handling, cutting, assembling, and disposing of PT lumber:

- Wear gloves, long sleeves, safety goggles, and a dust mask or respirator when handling and cutting pressure-treated wood.
- Whenever possible, cut wood outdoors to avoid airborne sawdust and accumulations of it indoors.
- Do not burn PT lumber or scraps. All construction debris and sawdust should be collected and disposed of in regular trash collection.
- Treated wood should not come in direct or indirect contact with drinking water and any surface or structure where food is prepared or stored.
- Wash hands and other exposed areas thoroughly before eating, drinking, using the bathroom, or using tobacco products. Wash work clothing separately from other laundry.
- The copper-base treatments corrode fasteners and hardware. Over time, this can result in loss of strength in your deck. The industry recommends using triple-coated, hot-dipped, galvanized connectors and fasteners that meet ASTM standard A153. Stainless-steel hardware is acceptable, and coated exterior fasteners may be suitable; check the manufacturer's recommendations. Connectors should be made of ASTM A653 Class G 185 material or better (1.85 oz./zinc per square foot). Make sure connectors are rated for treated lumber. Aluminum flashing, hardware, or fasteners should never be used with the copper-base preservatives.
- PT lumber rated for ground contact requires stainless-steel fasteners and connectors. Dry wood and wood treated with waterproofing might slow the rate of corrosion, but in all cases fasteners and connectors should be inspected regularly.

FRAMING LUMBER

2×6   2×8   2×10   2×12

Exotic species

For those who want something special, there are more exotic species, such as ipe, cambara, and meranti. These species are more durable, more difficult to work, and more expensive. Make sure you purchase them from a sustainable-forest supplier.

In general, pressure-treated lumber provides greater structural strength and is less expensive than other deck materials. Use it to frame the structure, then choose another material, such as cedar or redwood, for exposed surfaces like the decking and railings. If you apply a finish to any wood, test it on scrap before you make your final choice. Natural aging usually takes a few months with cedar or redwood, a year or two with pressure-treated lumber.

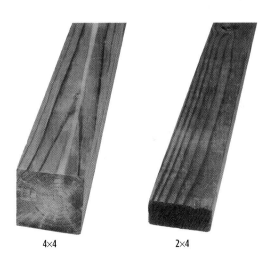

4×4   2×4

 BUYER'S GUIDE

CLOSER LOOK

SAPWOOD AND HEARTWOOD
Redwood and cedar look better than PT lumber, but only the heartwood naturally resists rot. The light-colored sapwood may rot in a few years unless treated regularly with preservative.

NOMINAL LUMBER SIZES
Lumber is identified by its nominal size, which is its rough dimension before it is trimmed to finished size at the lumber mill. Actual sizes are approximate lumber dimensions after trimming.

Nominal Size	Actual Size
1×4	¾"×3½"
1×6	¾"×5½"
2×2	1½"×1½"
2×4	1½"×3½"
2×6	1½"×5½"
2×8	1½"×7¼"
2×10	1½"×9¼"
4×4	3½"×3½"

Selecting the right boards

T he best way to get lumber you will be happy working with is to select the boards yourself and inspect each one. This way you can avoid having to deal with boards that are warped or otherwise defective when you build your deck.

The illustrations on this page show the kind of defects you should leave on the lumber rack.

◀ WARPS AND TWISTS
Reject boards with severe warps or twists. Warped boards have an evenly curved surface. Diagonal corners curl on twisted boards.

▼ LOOK DOWN THE LENGTH OF A BOARD TO CHECK FOR WARPS AND TWISTS
Also check for a crowned (curved) edge. Some boards may have a slight bow that will make the middle of the board higher than the ends. Mark this edge and install it upward. The board will straighten over time.

▶ SURFACE FLAWS
Reject boards with insect holes, rot, mildew, or sap pockets.

◀ MILL DAMAGE
Look for marks left by milling machines when the lumber was made. Reject the board unless you can cut off the damaged part and still have a usable length.

▼ CHECKS AND SPLITS
Look for checks and splits. A check is a crack going partway through the lumber; a split goes completely through. Cut off the damaged portion.

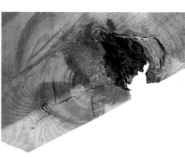

▼ WANE
Cut off a portion with untrimmed bark (called a wane). If the board has a good face and two good edges, it's OK to place the wane facedown.

▲ EXAMINE EVERY KNOT
Tight knots usually are acceptable. Don't use boards with knots at the edges for framing. Cut off portions with loose or missing knots. Also remove knots that are surrounded by dark rings—they may fall out later.

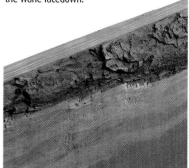

crown

BOARD WIDTH

Measure the width of each board before cutting and installing. Don't assume boards are the named size. There may be as much as ⅜-inch difference between two boards of the same nominal dimension—especially in pressure-treated lumber.

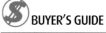

WORK SMARTER

STORING LUMBER

When your lumber arrives from your home center, you'll need to store it so it doesn't get wet or so it can dry out if it does.

Lay the boards out on pressure-treated posts and stack them in layers separated by 1× or 2× stock. Cover the stack with a tarp if the forecast calls for rain.

BUYER'S GUIDE

GOOD GRADES

Lumber grades No. 1 and No. 2 are usually recommended for decking. Although grade No. 1 is a little more expensive, it has fewer knots and flaws and should be less susceptible to warping and twisting, which means you'll have fewer problems and a more uniform-looking deck.

CLOSER LOOK

LUMBER IS GRADED

According to a number of criteria—number and kind of knots, overall appearance, and strength. For structural members like posts, beams, and joists, choose a No. 2 grade or lumber graded as Standard. For decking and railings get Select grades if you can afford it. Choose the best your budget will allow. A grade stamp will also indicate the quality of the stock and note its moisture content. For framing, air dried lumber is adequate. Use S-dry or MC-15 lumber for decking and rails.

DECKING GRADE STAMP

- Grade
- Radius-edge decking
- Grading association (Southern Pine Inspection Bureau)
- Seasoning (kiln dried, 19 percent moisture content)
- Producer
- Heat treated
- Mill number
- Southern Forest Products Association logo

CEDAR GRADE STAMP

- Producer
- Grade
- Species (Western red cedar)
- Seasoning (Green or unseasoned, moisture content greater than 19 percent)

Synthetic materials

If you're looking for decking material that's easy to install, cuts like wood, won't rot, and is virtually maintenance free, then you're looking for synthetic decking. Consumer demand has spurred technological innovations, and manufacturers have developed a number of synthetic materials that are fast becoming the most popular products in the deck business.

Synthetic materials come in several forms. Composites, vinyl, fiberglass-reinforced decking, and extruded thermoplastic materials are becoming more widely used because they don't suffer most of wood's frequent defects, including splitting, splintering, warping, and deteriorating. Synthetics, however, are not strong enough to be structural members—joists, posts, and beams.

Most composite materials are made from recycled wood byproducts (like wood chips and sawdust) and plastics (like recycled plastic grocery bags). Molded and compressed under heat with other resins, they form a material whose surface is slightly matted to the touch or stamped in a wood-grain pattern. Some manufacturers make decking with both a matte side and a wood-grain side. You can choose whichever suits your style. Some manufacturers even introduce chips of aromatic cedar into the decking so it smells like real wood.

Installation of most composites relies on the same techniques as installation of wood decking—with nails or screws predrilled into the decking. Some products are girder shaped and are installed with blind screws and invisible clip fasteners.

Some composites are made to fade over time—some into the natural-looking gray of real wood. If fading is an issue for you, choose a brand that has proven colorfast. Composites will even take paint and a few can be stained. Use latex-based paints and stains on these materials. Oil-based products won't stick.

Made from 100 percent polystyrene plastic and extruded into all of the shapes associated with decking materials (rails, post caps, and the like), thermoplastics are warrantied not to fade, rot, or otherwise show signs of deterioration for 25 years.

▼ **STYLE AND DURABILITY**
Composite decking looks as good as real wood but requires less maintenance.

Matte side

Textured side

Working with synthetics

All synthetic materials can be worked with standard woodworking tools, but manufacturers recommend using a carbide-tipped blade with 24 teeth or less when cutting this material. Drill pilot holes for screws with standard twist drills.

General considerations

Synthetic decking comes in a variety of forms and thicknesses. Most common are $\frac{5}{4}$ decking and 1½-inch extruded girders. Products are designed to comply with most building codes, but some localities may not allow synthetic materials. Always check with your local building code officials when planning to use synthetics. See pages 116–120 for information about installing synthetic decking, pages 159–161 for railing installation.

DESIGN TIP

MATCHING COLORS
There can be quite a bit of difference in the color of your synthetic decking and the joists under it. Don't wait until the color difference is noticeable and annoying. After you install the joists, paint them with an exterior paint that matches the color of your decking. You don't have to spend hours matching the color exactly. A close match will do. Even black will hide the joists between the spaces.

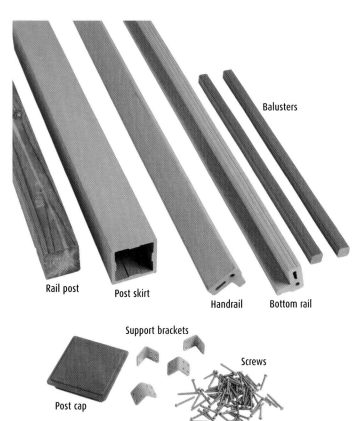

Rail post   Post skirt   Balusters   Handrail   Bottom rail

Support brackets

Screws

Post cap

◀ RAILINGS

Synthetic materials are made for stylish railings too. Some manufacturers offer a variety of styles and colors, all to match their decking materials.

▲ FANCY PATTERNS

Synthetic materials are just as adept at creating fancy railing patterns as wood. Some synthetic railings go together with screws using wood-style joints; others come with special brackets and hardware.

▶ AMENITIES

Let your imagination create other amenities for your deck with synthetic materials. Most are perfectly suited for constructing planters and seating.

▲ CURVES

The intrinsic flexibility of many synthetic products lends itself to a whole host of dramatic design effects, like this set of wide, curved steps.

Typical spans for synthetic decking

Decking Size	Loading: 100psf	
	Span	
⁵⁄₄× 6	16"	
2×4, 6, 8	24"	
2×6 stairs	16"	

Most synthetic decking must span at least three joists.

WORK SMARTER

BEARING AN EXTRA LOAD?
Hot tubs, spas, deck ponds, and even planters will add loads to your deck for which span tables do not account. Some structures like these will require beefed-up framing and possibly a concrete pad for support. If your deck plans call for any of these amenities, consult a local structural engineer or building code official for information about structural requirements.

▲ CHOOSE CAREFULLY

Some materials more closely resemble wood tones than others and offer more design options, so research the available materials carefully. Costs may be initially higher, but over the life of the deck you will save time and money in reduced maintenance.

Railing options to complement a deck

A wide variety of post, rail, and baluster styles are available that can be used with any railing. Choose those that best complement your overall deck design—ideally, with some aspect of its shape or construction that mirrors other decorative elements of your house and landscape.

Railing posts come in several lengths. Standard posts have flat faces on all four sides. Milled post faces are cut in decorative patterns—something you can do yourself if you have basic woodworking tools and skills. A separate post cap or finial (a decorative knob-like attachment) can be attached to the top of a standard post.

Besides basic 2×4 and 2×6 rail arrangements, rails are available with milled decorative profiles. Choose one that matches the post and baluster style. Rails are often precut (or can be) so that 2×2 balusters fit into a rabbet or channel on the inside. Graspable handrails are often required on stairs by local code. Codes may specify maximum dimensions for the size of the handrail.

Standard balusters with flat faces are made from 2×2 lumber. Some have a precut mitered end. Several decorative profiles are available in milled balusters. Another popular baluster is made from coated metal tubing (see pages 156–158).

POSTS

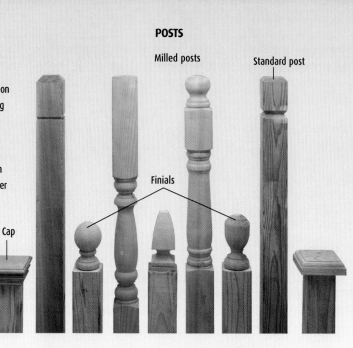

Milled posts

Standard post

Finials

Cap

RAILS

2×4/2×6

Milled rails

Graspable handrails

BALUSTERS

Coated metal

Milled balusters

Standard 2×2

Felt, flashing, and footings

Lumber and hardware are not the only materials you'll need to buy for your deck. You'll need 15-pound felt paper to reline the sheathing after you've cut away the siding to make room for the ledger.

You'll also need flashing to keep the rain from getting behind the ledger and rotting the sheathing. And, of course, you'll need materials with which to make footings.

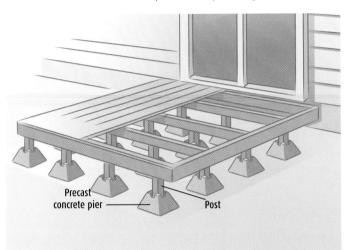

Precast concrete pier — Post

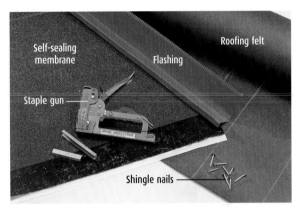

Self-sealing membrane — Roofing felt — Flashing — Staple gun — Shingle nails

FLOATING-FOUNDATION DECK SYSTEMS

Floating deck systems rely on a series of piers to support the deck structure. They speed deck construction because you don't have to dig or pour footings. See page 176 for installation instructions.

BARRIER MATERIALS

Install moisture and vapor barriers to protect deck and house framing. Place building paper behind a ledger when you remove existing siding material (see page 55). Attach strips of self-sealing membrane over the top seam between boards of built-up beams. Attach these materials with staples or shingle nails. Install flashing over the top edge of a ledger (see pages 55 and 59).

FOOTING MATERIALS

Precast piers can support both joists and posts. For a post, install a post base in the center or purchase piers with the hardware already mounted.

Precast concrete piers can be used with or without footings, depending on local codes. When used without hardware, as shown here, they simplify construction of ground-level decks.

Prefab fiber tubes form the concrete in footings. Although the tubes are sturdy enough to resist the pressures of concrete, you can cut them easily with a handsaw.

Plastic forms with a flared end are made for the base of footings. As you pour the footing, the concrete assumes the shape of the cone and provides a stable base.

You'll get about three footings from four 90-pound bags of **premix concrete**. For larger projects, mix your own with a power mixer or call in the ready-mix truck.

Precast concrete piers — Prefab fiber tubes — Premix concrete

Selecting fasteners

t goes without saying that you should always use corrosion-resistant fasteners when building your deck. The question is, "Which type of corrosion resistance is the best?" If you're using cedar, redwood, or another naturally resistant species, double-coated hot-dipped galvanized (HDG) connectors and fasteners are sufficient. Pressure-treated lumber requires triple-coated connectors and fasteners or those made from stainless steel (page 28). Ask the advice of your retailer when you buy deck fasteners. Fasteners should penetrate framing to a depth at least twice the thickness of the piece they fasten.

10d spiral nails

10d galvanized box nails

8d finish nails

TYPES OF DECK NAILS
Nails are common fasteners for decking material. You can use box nails for framing, spiral-shank or ringshank nails for decking, and finish nails for trim.

COMPOSITE DECK SCREWS
Made to pull the shavings into the hole in composite decking and prevent mushrooming around the head in synthetic material.

EXTERIOR-GRADE COATED DECK SCREWS
You can use #8 or #10 screws 2½ or 3½ inches long (depending on the material) for most deck work. Decking screws are made with a phillips drive, square drive, or combination head. Square drive heads won't strip out as easily.

TRIM-HEAD SCREWS
Made with smaller, less-obtrusive heads, but provide sufficient holding power for some applications, especially those in which you want to make the fastener less visible, like railings or trim work.

INVISIBLE FASTENERS

Decking clips are made with points that drive into the wood, holding the decking securely. Deck ties fit between the boards or slip into slots cut in the side of the decking and are screwed to the joists. Track systems fasten to the joists and decking from below.

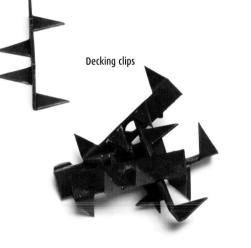

Decking clips

Deck ties

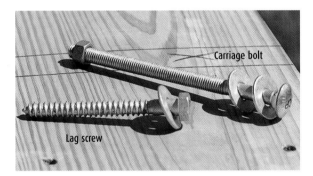

Carriage bolt

Lag screw

LAG SCREWS AND CARRIAGE BOLTS

These are large-diameter screws used to fasten framing. Large-diameter bolts also are used when there is access to both ends of the fastener. Carriage bolts have a rounded head which imparts a finished look to the connection. Machine bolts have a hexagonal-sided head similar to that on lag screws. Choose a bolt length at least 1 inch longer than the combined thickness of the pieces to be bolted together.

🕮 WORK SMARTER

WHAT SIZE FASTENER?

The longer and thicker a nail is, the better it holds. However, if a nail is too thick for the stock, it will split the wood and have almost no holding power at all. Although it might seem that building a deck calls for a wide selection of fasteners, those listed below will get you through most projects.

- Common, spiral, or ringshank nails (10d or 16d) for framing in 2× or thicker stock
- Box or ring shanknails (8d or 10d) in 1× or thinner stock
- Finish nails (8d or 10d) for applying trim
- Decking screws—#8 or #10, in appropriate lengths

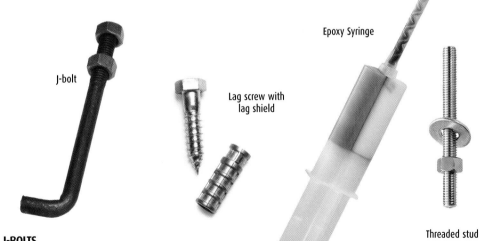

J-bolt

Epoxy Syringe

Lag screw with lag shield

Threaded stud

J-BOLTS

J-bolts are inserted in the footing when the concrete is wet and provide a strong connector for posts bases. The threads of the bolt are left exposed above the footing so the nut can anchor the post base to the cured concrete.

MASONRY ANCHORS

Inserting a threaded stud into a hole drilled into a concrete footing and filled with structural epoxy provides a solid connection for a post base. Threaded stock comes in precut lengths in ½- and ⅜-inch diameters with a nut and washer. To anchor lumber to a masonry wall, use a lag shield with a lag screw. The shield expands against the masonry in the sides of the hole as the lag screw is tightened.

2

TOOLS AND MATERIALS

Choosing framing connectors

Metal framing connectors make the strongest connection between framing members. Many local codes require their use, and special connectors are necessary in earthquake and hurricane zones. Attach connectors with fasteners specified by the manufacturer; never use roofing nails. Fill each hole in the connector with a fastener. When using framing connectors with pressure-treated lumber, follow the connector manufacturer's recommendations for corrosion resistance.

ADJUSTABLE POST BASE
Attaches post to footing, allows adjustment of position on footing, raises post end above ground.

POST CAP
Attaches beam to top of post. Made for a variety of post and beam sizes.

ADJUSTABLE POST CAP
Attaches beam to top of post, adjustable to fit different beam sizes.

RAFTER/HURRICANE TIE
Attaches 2× joist or rafter to the supporting member.

SEISMIC/HURRICANE TIE
Attaches 2× joist or rafter to the supporting member.

JOIST HANGER
Attaches 2× joist to face of ledger or beam, available for single and double joists and 45-degree angles.

SLOPEABLE AND SKEWABLE JOIST HANGER
Attaches 2× joist to framing, slope and side angle are adjustable.

ANGLE BRACKET
Angle bracket reinforces corner joints. Also available for angles other than 90 degrees.

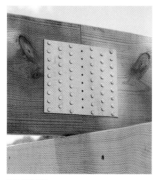

TIE PLATE
Also known as a nailing plate, reinforces spliced joint between two pieces of lumber.

T-STRAP
Reinforces joint between framing members. This type of connector is not a substitute for a post cap.

STAIR ANGLE
Attaches stair tread to stair stringer.

Basic hand tools

O ne of the reasons building a deck is a great home improvement project is that it doesn't require expensive tools. If you've done a few DIY projects, you'll probably have most of the tools you need already. If it's your first project, here's an opportunity to build a basic tool kit.

Mason's line, a **line level**, a **plumb bob**, and a **water level** are used in laying out footing positions and keeping things plumb and level. You'll also need a **tape measure** to take measurements. Always use the same one throughout the project—there may be discrepancies between different tape measures. For a large deck you'll need a **50- to 100-foot tape.**

A **layout square,** a **framing square,** a **bevel gauge,** and a long **straightedge** are used for layout and marking. A **layout square** makes quick work of accurately marking lumber for straight or angled cuts. Mark long lines by snapping a **chalk line**. A **level** helps level and plumb framing—get both a 2-foot and 4-foot model. A **post level** makes quick work out of keeping posts perfectly vertical in two planes. A **laser level** can also make deck layout easier and more accurate.

A **16-ounce** (minimum) **framing hammer** drives nails better than smaller models. Set nail heads with a **nail set.** Pound stakes with a **small sledge.**

Line level

Plumb bob and mason's line

50- to 100-foot tape measure

Chalk line

Bevel gauge

20- to 30-foot tape measure

Laser level

Post level

Layout square

Straightedge

Carpenters level

Install lag screws and nuts on hex-head or carriage bolts with a **combination wrench** or **socket wrench.**

Use a **pry bar** as a lever to shift lumber positions. A **cat's paw** is used for removing embedded nails. A long **pinch bar** (like a heavy, straight crowbar) breaks up hard soil to make excavation easier.

A **utility knife** has many uses on any building project, from trimming wood to marking for cut lines. A **chisel** and **handsaw** often are necessary for cutting notches or completing power saw cuts. Cut flashing with **aviation snips.** Apply

caulk with a **caulk gun.** A throwaway **foam brush** is useful for applying preservative to freshly cut surfaces on pressure-treated lumber. Sweep sawdust from deck surfaces with a **stiff-bristle push broom.** You can also use it to texture the surface of a ground-level concrete pad. A pair of **sawhorses** is useful for supporting lumber. Several **clamps** will be helpful for holding lumber in position.

Safety gear you should have on hand: **safety glasses or goggles, earplugs or earmuff protectors,** a **dust mask,** and **work gloves and boots.**

Framing hammer

Utility knife

Framing square

Small sledge

Nail set

Quick clamp

Chisel

Wrenches

Foam brushes

Handsaw

Socket wrench

Caulk gun

Pry bar

Aviation snips

Cat's paw

Sawhorse

Stiff-bristle push broom

Basic power tools

You may already have many of the basic power tools necessary for deck building. Building a deck can give tools a workout, so make sure yours are in good condition.

If your circular saw won't cut straight, try replacing and squaring the blade. If your cordless drill wobbles when you use it, the chuck may be worn out. If your saber saw vibrates excessively, the drive shaft or blade may be bent.

Whether you're replacing or buying new, buy the best you can afford. In general, the lower the amperage or voltage in cordless tools, the less power a tool will have. As with hand tools, keep power tools and accessories clean, dry, and rust-free. Sharp saw blades and drill bits work better and are safer to use than dull blades and bits.

Power tools you'll need: The workhorse for deck building is a **circular saw.** A saw with a 7¼-inch (see page 48) blade is easy to handle and has the capacity

for the job. Use a **power mitersaw** for miter cuts and when many straight crosscuts are needed. A compound sliding mitersaw is the handiest kind to have. A **jigsaw** makes smooth cuts in tight areas. Use a **reciprocating saw** for making cuts in framing that can't be cut with a circular saw.

It's handy to have both a **cordless drill/driver** and a **corded drill**. A cordless drill/driver provides freedom of movement. Buy one in a kit with two batteries and a quick charger. The drill/driver has a clutch you can set to drive screws to the correct depth. A corded drill provides continuous power when you have a lot of holes to drill. Make holes in concrete with a **hammer drill**. Drills use an assortment of drill bits and screw tips. A hammer drill uses larger heavy-duty masonry bits that are ideal for making holes in concrete.

Use a GFCI-protected extension cord when operating corded power tools outdoors.

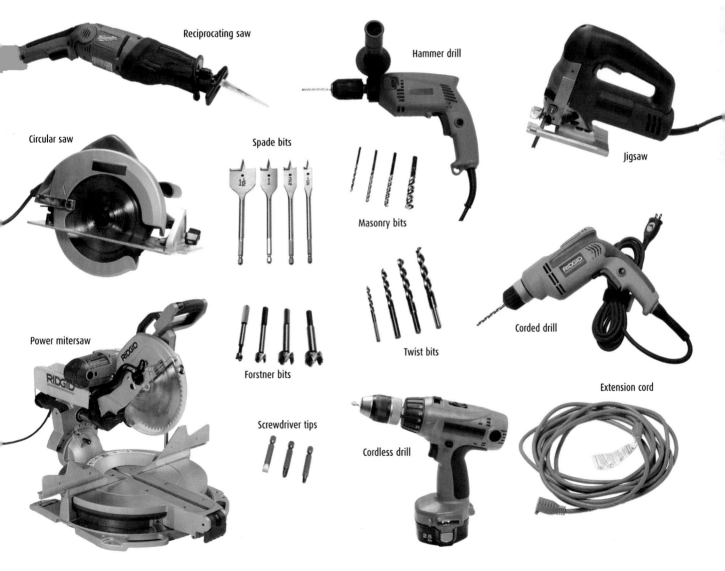

Reciprocating saw

Hammer drill

Jigsaw

Circular saw

Spade bits

Masonry bits

Power mitersaw

Forstner bits

Twist bits

Corded drill

Screwdriver tips

Cordless drill

Extension cord

Measuring, marking, squaring, and plumbing

T hese four activities are essential to all home construction projects. If you can perform them accurately and without hesitation, you're well on your way to success in deck building.

An old carpenter's adage is appropriate here: "Measure twice, cut once." This applies not only to taking measurements, but also to the other three activities. Double-check all your work with squares, measuring tapes, and levels before cutting, drilling, or putting in fasteners.

Point of the V indicates the precise spot.

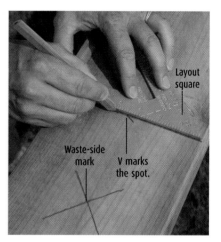

Layout square

Waste-side mark — V marks the spot.

MARKING A CROSSCUT

Marking for a crosscut is a three-step operation. First square the end of the board you'll be cutting. Then hook the tape measure on the end of the board and extend the tape until you reach the length for the crosscut. Make a V mark with a sharp pencil. Mark

the waste side of the board with a large X. Hold the point of the pencil on the point of the V, and slide a layout square along the edge of the board until it touches the pencil tip without moving it. Draw a straight cutting line along the edge of the square.

Square

Check level with center vial.

STANLEY FatMax

SQUARE BOARDS WITH A FRAMING SQUARE

Hold the square inside or outside the joint and look along the lengths of both the tongue (short side) and the blade (long side). If you see light anywhere along either edge of the square, pull or push one or both of the boards until the square fits snugly.

CARPENTER'S LEVEL

Use a 4-foot carpenter's level to level framing whenever you have room for its length. Shorter levels may be thrown off by warps or waves in the boards. Boards are level when the bubble is centered in the vial.

WATER LEVEL

Make a mark at the water level line in the tubing. Double-check that the water level line at the other end of the tubing is still aligned with the leveling point. Slowly raise or lower the free end to adjust water level lines, if necessary.

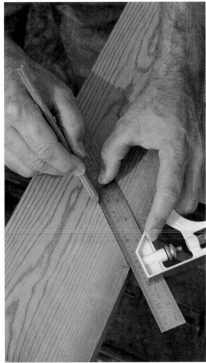

MARKING A RIP CUT

Begin by marking the width of the cut on both ends of the board. Then hook a chalk line tightly on the marks and snap the line. If the cut runs parallel to the edge of the board, draw the cut line by holding a pencil against a square at the proper width. Pull the square and pencil down the length of the board.

MARKING A 45-DEGREE MITER

Miter cuts are angled cuts and are most often made at 45 degrees. Start by measuring the longer side of the miter and setting your combination square or layout square on that mark. Then draw the cut line.

MARKING ANGLES OTHER THAN 45 AND 90 DEGREES

Use a bevel gauge. Set the handle on the outside edge of the board and lock the blade. Then move the gauge to the place you want to cut, and mark the line.

ELECTRONIC WATER LEVEL

An electronic water level does the same things as a manual one, but it beeps when the water in both ends of the tube is on the same plane. Attach the unit on the level line and move the opposite end of the tube until the tone sounds.

LASER LEVEL

Make quick work out of establishing horizontal level lines with a laser level. Set the unit on a tripod and position it to throw the laser beam at the level point. Mark the position of the line with a carpenter's pencil.

POST LEVEL

Plumb posts in two planes at the same time with a post level. Strap the level to the post so you can watch the vials while you move the post. Brace the post when the bubbles in both vials are centered.

Circular saw

You'll use your circular saw more than any other tool when you're building your deck. Using the saw efficiently will make your work proceed much more quickly. If you're new to using this saw, or even just a bit rusty, save yourself time in the long run by practicing the cuts shown here on pieces of scrap. Always make sure you have a firm grip on the saw, always start the saw before pushing the blade into the cut, and always line the blade up so it cuts on the waste side of the line. Don't force the saw into the cut and if you get off the mark, don't try to force the saw back to the line. Back it up and reposition the blade. Always check your saw for square as shown below.

Sight on the guide or on the blade as you cut.

FREEHAND CUTS
These can be made quickly and accurately. Rest the edge of the board on a solid surface and tilt it. Line up the blade with the cut line, start the saw, and let gravity pull it down the line. Keep the saw plate flat on the stock as you cut.

GUIDED CROSSCUTS
Hold (or clamp) a layout square so the saw blade will line up with the cut line. Start the saw and push it with the saw plate tightly against the layout square.

Checking angles

SQUARING A CIRCULAR SAW
Unplug the saw and lower the baseplate until the blade extends fully. Set the foot of a layout square on the saw base. Slide the right-angle edge of the square against the side of the blade between carbide teeth. The side of the blade should be in contact with the edge of the square along its entire length. If it isn't, adjust the blade angle until it is and make a new '0' mark on the scale.

CHECK THE ANGLE
Check the angle of a 45-degree cut with a layout square. Adjust the position of the saw and recut the board.

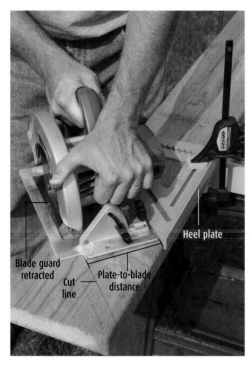

Blade guard retracted
Cut line
Plate-to-blade distance
Heel plate

TOOL SAVVY

CIRCULAR SAW SUPPORT
Support the motor of a circular saw to make the most accurate cuts, especially when making bevel cuts. It is difficult to control a saw when the base isn't fully supported. If you need to make a cut that requires leaving the saw base unsupported, flip the board to make the cut.

Front edge

Top

ACCURATE MITER CUTS
First measure the plate-to-blade distance. Clamp a layout square to the board and retract the blade guard. Start the saw and push it along the line. Cut the miter before you cut the board to length so you can recut the miter if you make a mistake.

Rip guide

RIP CUT PARALLEL TO THE EDGE OF A BOARD
Attach a rip guide to the saw plate. If the cut is not parallel to the edge, either mark it and cut it freehand or clamp a long straightedge as a guide. Don't force the saw away from the cut—the rip guide might flex with it.

THE STRAIGHT STORY
Long straight cuts are difficult to make accurately with a circular saw. Make a cutting guide with a long straightedge and a couple of clamps. If the clamps interfere with the saw, cut from the opposite direction or move the clamps slightly. Or buy a straightedge saw guide that is self-clamping and available in various lengths.

Spacer
Workpiece
Work support

CUTTING LONG STOCK

Support the board on both sides of the cut so the saw won't bind or kick back. If the waste side is longer than 2 feet, support the board in four places. That way both sides of the cut will stay put and you can make a straight, neat cut.

BUYER'S GUIDE

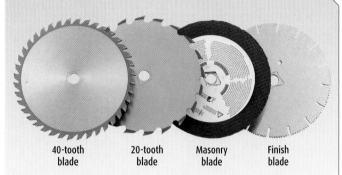

40-tooth blade | 20-tooth blade | Masonry blade | Finish blade

THE BEST BLADES MAKE THE BEST CUTS

Choose the best 7¼-inch circular saw blade for the cutting you do: A **40-tooth carbide-tip blade** makes clean-edge miter cuts, bevel cuts, and crosscuts (cutting across the board grain). A **20-tooth carbide-tip blade** is for general cutting. A **masonry blade** cuts concrete and stucco. A **finish blade** makes very smooth cuts in fascia and for other visible joints. Use a metal cutting blade, made from material similar to that used in a masonry blade but marked as a blade for metal, to cut metal siding. The tooth count is higher for miter saws. For example, a 10-inch blade for general cutting has 30 to 40 teeth. Don't use a masonry blade in a mitersaw.

BUYER'S GUIDE

GET THE RIGHT (OR LEFT) SAW

Circular saws are available with the saw blade mounted on either the right or left side of the motor (near right). A right-handed person using a saw with a blade on the right side must look over the saw body to see the cutting path (far right). This is awkward and may cause inaccurate cuts. If you buy a new saw, purchase one that fits the way you work. Cordless circular saws are good for making cuts in tight spaces, though they don't work for cutting many boards. **Purchase the best saw you can afford. Pick the tool up and test it for fit**—some saws may be too heavy for you to safely and comfortably use.

Using a compound mitersaw

Using a compound mitersaw is the easiest way to make one cut that is a combination of bevel and miter angles. This type of cut is common when installing a railing or other structure at an angle other than 90 degrees to the deck. A compound mitersaw is more expensive than a power mitersaw but it can be rented.

 **REAL WORLD**

MAKE CONSISTENT CUTS
If you can't understand why your boards are always just a little bit short no matter how accurately you measure, the problem may be in your cuttting rather than your measuring. If you consistently cut pieces $\frac{1}{16}$ to $\frac{1}{8}$ inch short, you're probably cutting on the wrong side of the line. Instead of cutting down the middle of the marked cutting line, saw on the waste side of it. Then you'll probably find that everything fits together perfectly!

1 **MARK THE CUTTING LINES**
Mark a cutting line on a scrap board of the same dimension as the one that will be installed. Shown at right is an angled stair railing installation. Temporarily position the scrap board. Determine both angles at which it must be cut. The angle of the board relative to vertical will be the miter angle of the saw blade. The angle of the board relative to horizontal will be the bevel angle of the blade. Use a bevel gauge if necessary (see page 45).

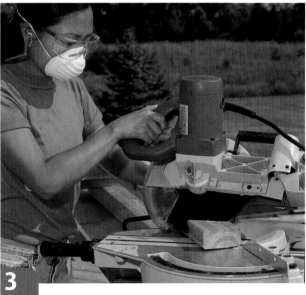

2 **MAKE A TEST CUT**
Make the cut on a scrap piece of board after setting the miter and bevel angles of the saw blade. Cut about ¼ inch on the waste side of the line to see if the cut lines up correctly. Test fit the scrap piece. Make adjustments as necessary until the test piece fits properly.

3 **MAKE THE COMPOUND CUT**
Cut the board with the blade at its final settings from Step 2. After you've cut the miter, hold the board in position on the deck and mark its length. Then cut the board on this mark.

Using a reciprocating saw

KEEP SHOE IN CONTACT

Rest the base of the saw shoe against the piece to be cut. This controls the cut and prevents vibration. Use a blade long enough to pass completely through the lumber. Mount the blade with the teeth facing up to get into tight spots.

REVERSE THE BLADE

Make cuts against obstacles by mounting the blade in the saw so the teeth face up. Rest the base of the saw shoe against the piece to be cut. Cut carefully so the blade doesn't damage other materials.

BUYER'S GUIDE

THE RIGHT RECIPROCATING SAW BLADE FOR THE JOB
Choose the proper reciprocating saw blade for the cut you make. **Blades with fewer teeth cut faster but make rougher cuts. More teeth means a slower, smoother cut.** Some blades are intended for cutting nail-embedded wood. Blades with many tiny teeth make cuts in metal. Thin blades are more flexible, but thick blades provide more control and straighter cuts. Wide blades are stronger but can't make cuts with tight curves. Narrow blades easily cut contours.

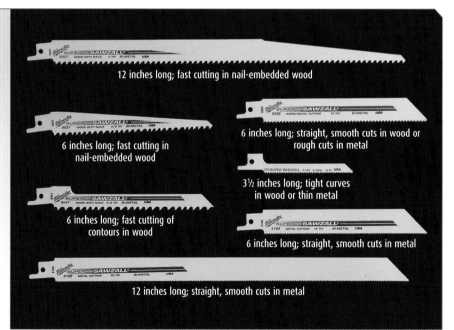

12 inches long; fast cutting in nail-embedded wood

6 inches long; fast cutting in nail-embedded wood

6 inches long; straight, smooth cuts in wood or rough cuts in metal

3½ inches long; tight curves in wood or thin metal

6 inches long; fast cutting of contours in wood

6 inches long; straight, smooth cuts in metal

12 inches long; straight, smooth cuts in metal

Setting up the work site

Set up a work area for greatest efficiency and accuracy. Make a saw platform from sawhorses and 2× lumber (below, left). Place cutting supports about 3 feet from each side of the saw. The tops of the supports should be level with the saw table surface. Use a portable roller support stand and workstand when cutting long pieces of lumber (right). The height of the stand is adjustable and the roller makes positioning the lumber easy.

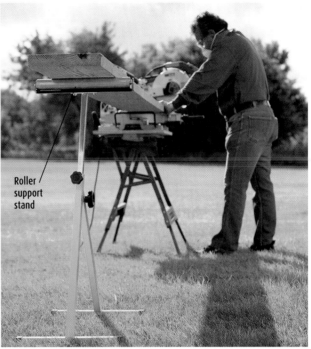

Roller support stand

SAFETY ALERT

SAFETY GEAR

Use appropriate safety gear and follow proper safety procedures when building a deck:

- Wear hearing and eye protection when using all power tools.
- Wear eye protection when using striking tools.
- Wear a dust mask when cutting lumber and mixing concrete.
- Wear gloves and work boots when handling lumber and concrete. (DO NOT wear gloves when operating power saws.)
- Use GFCI-protected power cords for power tools outdoors.

Secure a ladder carefully before using it. Make certain both feet are firmly planted. Drive stakes on the down-grade side of the feet (above, left) if there is any slope to the ground. Strap or rope the top end of a ladder to framing or another unmovable object when more than 8 feet from the ground (above, right). Or use a ladder support, a wide piece that attaches to the top of the ladder, to brace the ladder against the house. Make sure that your weight, plus whatever you carry up the ladder, doesn't exceed the maximum safe load for the ladder. Scaffolding is a more stable and safer option for working high off the ground. It's relatively inexpensive to rent and also makes work easier and quicker.

Laying out a deck

he best way to make sure that all of the elements of your deck fit together precisely is to take your time and do careful layout work. The effort will pay off—you'll have a deck that looks professionally built and can stand up to both the elements and the rigors of outdoor activities.

This book shows the logical progression of work when you build a deck. To keep the project moving smoothly, take the steps in order. Make a construction schedule listing the tasks you have to complete and when you intend to complete them. Here are the tasks in order:

- Choose materials
- Pick deck location
- Draw plans
- Estimate material quantities and costs
- Apply for building permit and schedule inspections
- Order materials
- Set up workstation and organize materials
- Prepare site
- Install ledger

Chapter 3 highlights

INSTALLING A LEDGER
This is the board that you attach to the house to bear the weight of the deck and connect it to the house.

54

LAYING OUT FOOTINGS
Laying out footings in a straight line is the key to a structure that's easy to build and long lasting.

62

LAYOUT OPTIONS FOR SMALL DECKS
Laying out small structures is really quick and easy with a few techniques from the carpenter's trick bag.

66

LAYING OUT A FREESTANDING DECK
Freestanding decks offer a host of design possibilities you can't accomplish with any other design.

67

- Lay out site
- Pour footings and set posts
- Install beams and joists
- Lay decking
- Build railings and stairs

Finish each step before tackling the next one. At the end of each work day, put everything away so you won't have to hunt for materials or tools. Have a contingency plan; rainy days may interrupt the schedule, for instance, or you may encounter unforeseen situations that cause delays.

Have lumber delivered a couple of weeks before you build to let it dry out (especially pressure-treated stock). Cover it with plastic so it stays dry while it adjusts to local moisture conditions. If your project includes a concrete pad that requires a large amount of concrete, arrange for ready-mix concrete. You could schedule the pad installation so the concrete for it is delivered at the same time as the concrete for footings.

Once you begin the layout, keep children and pets out of the project area. Although batterboards, strings, and spikes make a tempting playground, for the safety of all concerned make the work site off-limits.

Installing a ledger

PROJECT DETAILS

SKILLS: Cutting siding, flashing, and lumber; drilling holes; driving fasteners

PROJECT: Installing a 16-foot ledger, installing flashing, and attaching ledger

TIME TO COMPLETE

EXPERIENCED: 3 hrs.
HANDY: 4 hrs.
NOVICE: 5 hrs.

STUFF YOU'LL NEED

TOOLS: Hammer, tape measure, zip tool, chalk line, speed square, circular saw, level, drill, tin snips, caulk gun, ratchet and socket

MATERIALS: Lumber, building paper, fasteners, flashing, caulk

I nstalling a ledger on the house is the first step in laying out an attached deck. Freestanding decks don't require ledgers. The ledger, which is actually a header for the joists, establishes the height of the deck and transfers the weight of the deck to the foundation of the house. Attach the ledger so the surface of the installed decking will be at least 1 inch below the interior floor level to keep water and snowmelt from seeping into the house.

In most cases the ledger will be fastened to the band joist or wall studs with lag screws that penetrate the sheathing. Masonry foundations will require masonry anchors, and ledger sections that skirt a bay window may require additional support.

Although there are several ways to attach a ledger to the house, most of them require removing a section of the siding (metal, vinyl, or wood) in order to create a vertical surface on which the ledger rests. Building codes in some localities, however, may prohibit removal of the siding, so check your local codes before starting. In such cases, one of the alternate techniques shown on page 57 should meet code.

CUTAWAY VIEW

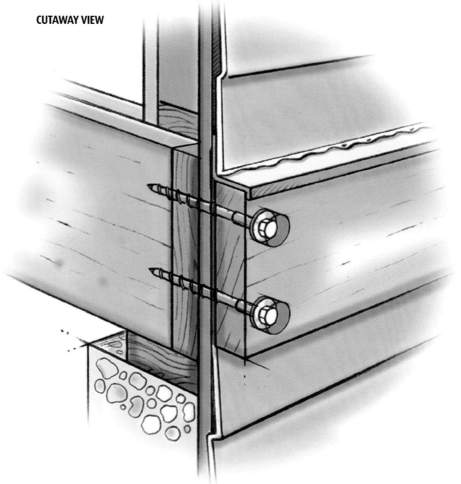

LEDGER ON SIDING

Remove a section of the siding material before attaching the ledger. You may need to use a zip tool (see "Tool Savvy" on the opposite page) to release the ends of the siding. Attach the ledger using lag screws driven into the band joist or studs.

Installing a ledger on siding

1

MARK THE LEDGER LOCATION
Mark the outline of the ledger so the top edge falls at least an inch below the exterior door. Extend the line with a level to mark the ends of the ledger, adding 1½ inches at each end to allow for the rim joists. Snap chalk lines to outline the position of the ledger.

2

CUT AWAY THE SIDING
Set the circular saw blade (a metal blade for vinyl or metal siding) to cut through the siding but not the sheathing. Cut just to the outside of the lines, stopping the blade when it touches the corners. Snip out the corners of vinyl or metal siding and remove it. Cut the corners of wood siding with a chisel.

3

INSTALL FLASHING
Slide galvanized flashing (often called Z-flashing) so at least 1 inch fits behind the siding. Pressure should keep it in place until you install the ledger. Notch the flashing to fit around door thresholds and make any overlaps at least 3 inches wide.

TOOL SAVVY

UNLOCKING SIDING JOINTS
Unlocking the joint between siding sections usually requires the use of a specialty siding tool called a zip tool. Using this tool will help prevent damage to the siding and allow you to get at the nails driven through the top flange. Insert the zip tool in the joint between two pieces (left) and slide it down the length of the pieces, releasing the hooked edge of the top piece from the nailed flange on the bottom piece. Do this at both top and bottom joints to remove a full piece of siding (right). Use this method to remove vinyl siding for cutting as an alternative to cutting it in place. Replace the siding after cutting it to fit around the ledger.

Installing a ledger on siding *(continued)*

4

LEVEL THE LEDGER

Cut the ledger to length, mark the location of the joists, and raise the ledger into the cutout. Center the ledger in the opening and drive one nail at the center of the top edge. Level the ledger and drive nails in the upper corners. Reinstall cut siding pieces along the bottom of the ledger, if necessary. Slide the upper edge of the siding underneath the ledger before driving the fasteners in the next step.

5

ATTACH THE LEDGER

Drill pilot holes and install the lag screws so they penetrate the sheathing and the house band joist by at least 1½ inches. Tighten each screw until the washer begins to compress the wood underneath.

WORK SMARTER

GOOD HELP WHEN YOU NEED IT
It's easier to have a helper when attaching a ledger to a house, but if you must work by yourself, use braces. Use braces even when you have a helper when attaching a ledger to masonry surfaces. Lean braces of scrap lengths of lumber against the house at an angle so they can support the ledger board. Lift the ledger onto the braces, then adjust each brace by moving the bottom end closer to or farther from the wall until the ledger is level. Leave the braces in place until you attach both ends of the ledger to the wall.

LAYING OUT A DECK

3

Optional ledger installations

Shimming the ledger

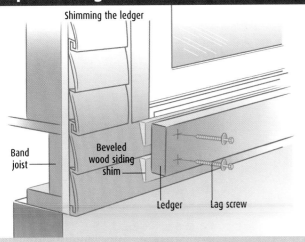

Band joist

Beveled wood siding shim

Ledger

Lag screw

Hold-off method

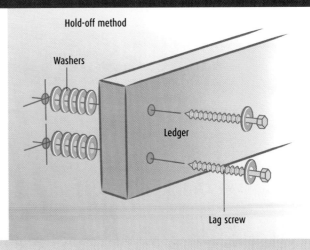

Washers

Ledger

Lag screw

Some local building codes allow ledgers to be shimmed to the surface of the siding. The shims keep the ledger vertical and make cutting the siding unnecessary. Cut shims from wooden siding stock and tack them upside down on your ledger location. Drill pilot holes and fasten the ledger to the band joist with lag screws.

If your local codes require a ledger be installed with its back edge held off the

siding (so it can dry out quickly), attach the ledger temporarily and drill all the fastener pilot holes, but do not install the lag screws. Remove the ledger, push the lag screws through the holes, and slip on four or five washers behind the ledger. Drive the screws into the pilot holes.

REAL WORLD

FLASHING PREVENTS WATER DAMAGE
Always install flashing over the ledger so it fits up underneath the siding. That wasn't done on this deck. Although the ledger board showed only a little water damage, this is the mess that developed behind the ledger. Sheathing and framing members had to be ripped out and replaced, taking much more time and money than installing flashing right in the first place.

WORK SMARTER

NOTCH FLASHING ON WOOD SIDING
Unlike metal and vinyl siding, you may have difficulty when you try to slide the flashing behind the wood siding above the ledger cutout. Depending on where you've made the ledger cutout, the flashing may be blocked by nails attaching the remaining siding to the house. Cut V-notches into the flashing at these spots to position it properly—at least 1 inch of the flashing must extend behind the siding.

Installing ledger boards on masonry

⊘ PROJECT DETAILS

SKILLS: Cutting lumber and flashing, drilling holes in concrete, driving fasteners

PROJECT: Installing a 16-foot ledger and flashing

🕐 TIME TO COMPLETE

EXPERIENCED: 3 hrs.
HANDY: 4 hrs.
NOVICE: 5 hrs.

✓ STUFF YOU'LL NEED

TOOLS: Hammer, tape measure, speed square, circular saw, level, hammer drill, tin snips, caulk gun, ratchet and socket

MATERIALS: Lumber, fasteners, epoxy, flashing, caulk

Like other ledger installations, a ledger mounted on concrete block or a concrete wall requires flashing. You can install the flashing in a kerf cut into the wall (see page 61) or insert it between the ledger and the wall and bend it to cover the top of the ledger. Masonry bolts or lag shields are an option to epoxied threaded studs for attaching the ledger.

CUTAWAY VIEW

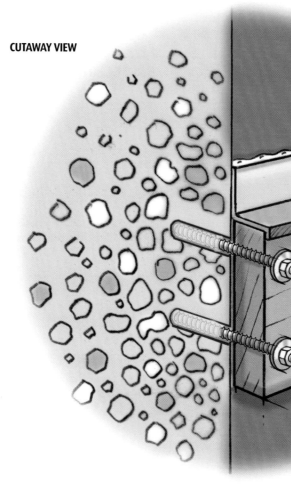

🔍 CLOSER LOOK

KNOW WHERE FASTENERS GO

Fasteners should penetrate a concrete block wall in the mortar joints (the seams between blocks) or in the webs (the solid portions of each block that surround the hollow core areas, called voids). Plan fastener positions for the mortar joints and adjust the ledger position if necessary unless you are confident of the web position (position depends on the type of concrete block used in the wall). Check local code regulations because there are different standards for where fasteners should be placed.

LEDGER BOARD ON MASONRY

Attaching a ledger to concrete is simple when using threaded studs, secured with epoxy, in holes drilled into the concrete wall. Since the stud requires the same diameter hole in the ledger and the wall, both holes are drilled after bracing the ledger into position.

3

LAYING OUT A DECK

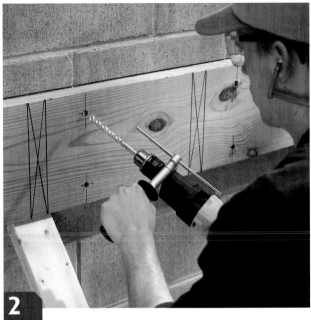

1 MARK THE LOCATION

Outline the position of the ledger on the concrete surface with a permanent marker. Because wall surface material isn't cut and removed, you don't need to allow space for the rim joists.

2 DRILL THE HOLES

Cut the ledger to length, mark the location of the joists, and prop the ledger in place. Make sure it's level and stays that way. Then drill pilot holes for the fasteners in the ledger. Change to a masonry bit of the same diameter as the wood bit and drill a 3-inch-deep hole into the concrete.

3 SQUEEZE IN THE EPOXY

Insert an epoxy screen into the hole (a round screen that gives the epoxy additional tooth in the hole and is made especially for this purpose). Following the manufacturer's instructions, push the recommended amount of structural epoxy into the hole. (One syringe usually contains enough epoxy for six holes.) Always wear gloves while handling epoxy—and follow the manufacturer's safety recommendations.

4 INSTALL THREADED STUD

Quickly insert a threaded stud into the hole. (You have only a few minutes before the epoxy begins to harden.) Let the epoxy harden completely (usually for 24 hours, depending on weather conditions), following manufacturer's directions.

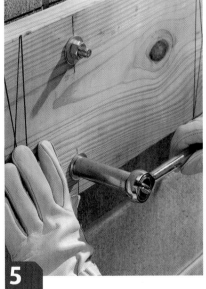

5 ATTACH LEDGER

Install a washer and nut on each stud and tighten until the washer compresses the wood underneath. Check the bolts after 24 hours and tighten if necessary. Apply a heavy bead of silicone caulk on the joint between the top edge of the ledger and the wall, and seat the metal flashing into it. Apply another bead of caulk along the joint at the top edge of the flashing.

Installing ledger boards on stucco

nstalling a ledger on stucco does not require removal of the stucco surface, but it does call for installation of flashing. The upper flange on the flashing is bent to fit into a shallow cut made in the stucco surface. You'll make the cut and slip in the flashing after you've hung the ledger. This requires you to countersink the heads of the lag screws so the circular saw doesn't get hung up on the fasteners. Otherwise the ledger is positioned and attached using the same techniques as you would for siding. Be sure to cut the flashing long enough to extend beyond the ends of the ledger so it will cover the rim joists and fascia.

Some local codes require that flashing be installed behind the stucco surface. This is a complicated job that you should leave to a professional contractor.

To keep the ledger as flat as possible, knock down large ridges or bumps in the stucco with glancing hammer blows. Easy does it—use too much force and the stucco may break up and fall off.

CUTAWAY VIEW

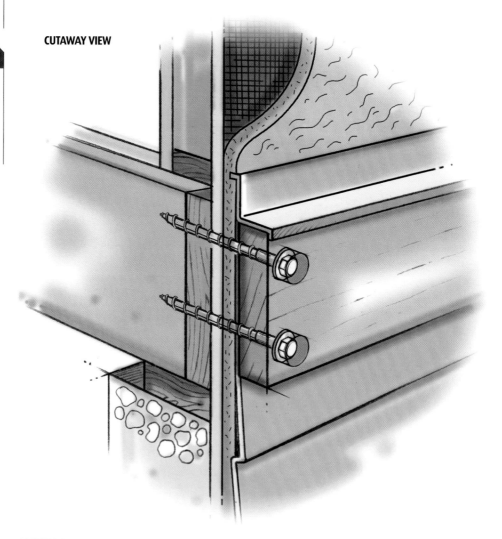

COUNTERSINK THE FASTENERS

Drill a countersunk hole wide and deep enough so the washer and head of each fastener will fit below the ledger surface. This is necessary so the fasteners won't interfere with a circular saw when you cut a kerf in the stucco. Drill pilot holes through the centers of the countersunk holes and install the fasteners. Use a masonry bit to cut through the stucco layer (usually less than 1 inch thick) after drilling through the ledger with a regular twist bit.

1

CUT A KERF IN THE STUCCO

Install the ledger, following the procedure on pages 58–59. Measure the height of the top flange on the metal flashing. Subtract ¼ inch from this measurement and mark a line at this distance above the top edge of the ledger. Attach a straight piece of level 1× stock to the ledger as a cutting guide. Using a masonry blade, cut a kerf in the stucco ⅜ inch deep.

2

INSTALL THE FLASHING

Clamp ¼ inch of the upper flange of the flashing between two lengths of 1× stock and bend the flashing so it forms a perpendicular lip. Push this lip into the kerf and snug up the flashing against the ledger. Make sure the flashing is firmly seated in the kerf along its entire length. Then apply silicone caulk to seal the flashing in the stucco. Also fill the countersunk holes with caulk.

🔍 CLOSER LOOK

ANGLE KEEPS VENT FLOWING

When you run into obstructions that fall along the length of the ledger, make cutouts to accommodate them. When notching for a vent, angle the bottom edge with a jigsaw so the airflow isn't restricted.

📖 WORK SMARTER

MAKING A LONG LEDGER

If you need a longer ledger than you can make with one board, cut additional lengths—each at least 3 feet long. Butt the sections together. If mounting a ledger to studs, center the joint on a stud. Drill pilot holes and drive screws on both sides of the splice into cleats you have installed inside on both sides of the stud. Most local codes also require the addition of a metal connector, such as a tie plate, at the splice (page 40).

Butt joint

Laying out footings

PROJECT DETAILS

SKILLS: Measuring, driving stakes and spikes, leveling string lines
PROJECT: Laying out footings for a 16×12-foot deck

TIME TO COMPLETE

EXPERIENCED: 3 hrs.
HANDY: 4 hrs.
NOVICE: 5 hrs.

STUFF YOU'LL NEED

TOOLS: Tape measure, small sledge, plumb bob, line level, mason's string
MATERIALS: Lumber, screws, landscape spikes, masking tape, colored marking tape

Once the ledger is in place, you can use it to locate the footings, laying out the site and footing locations with batterboards and mason's lines. Mason's line can be stretched tightly without breaking, and won't sag. Don't use a substitute. Batterboards must be rigid enough to stand straight against the tension of tightly pulled layout lines, so use stakes long enough to be driven securely into the ground.

WORK SMARTER

LEVEL YOUR LINE LEVEL
Position a line level within 12 inches of the end of a line for greatest accuracy. Although it weighs very little, placing the line level toward the middle of a line can make the line sag slightly, especially when the string is longer than 20 feet. A water level (see page 44) is more accurate for leveling across long distances.

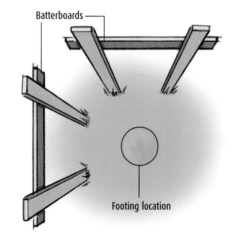

Batterboards

Footing location

LAY OUT BATTERBOARDS
Batterboards make a stable frame to support the mason's line used in laying out your site. Make each batterboard from two stakes (2×2s or 2×4s) and a 1×4 crosspiece. Make the stakes long enough (at least 2 feet long) and sharpen the ends. Attach the crosspiece to the stakes with screws. Drive the stakes into the ground so the crosspiece will be about 18 inches above grade.

1

MARK THE POST CENTER
Mark the center of the outside post location on the ledger. Partially drive a screw or nail at the bottom edge of the ledger at this mark to serve as a tie-off point for a plumb line.

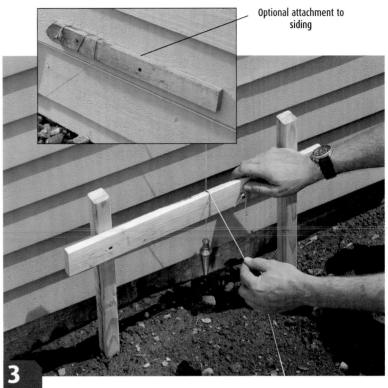

Optional attachment to siding

2
MARK THE POINT ON THE GROUND
Drop a plumb line from the center mark made in Step 1. This transfers the point to the ground accurately.

3
PUT IN BATTERBOARDS
Drive a batterboard near the wall at the bottom of the plumb line with the crosspiece level. If the ground slopes away from the house, install the crosspiece close enough to the ground so the batterboard at the opposite end will be no more than 3 feet high. Make a mark on the crosspiece aligned with the plumb line. Tie one end of the mason's line to a screw driven near the mark. Wrap the line several times around the crosspiece and line it up with the mark on the last wrap.

4
POSITION OUTER BATTERBOARDS
Position the batterboard for the outside corner about 3 feet beyond the location of the footing. You can either preassemble the batterboard or drive the batterboard stakes and attach the crosspiece as in the next step.

5
STRETCH THE LINE
Attach the crosspiece with one screw if you haven't preassembled it. Wrap the line at the center of the crosspiece and stretch it tight. Stretch the string until it is tight, level the line with a line level, and fasten the other end of the crosspiece with another screw. Install the remaining batterboards at the other corners.

6

SQUARE THE CORNERS

Stretch the lines tightly, and adjust the batterboards until the lines just touch at their intersections. Square the corners using the 3-4-5 triangle method (see opposite page).

7

MARK LINE LOCATIONS

Once the corners are square, mark each crosspiece where the line crosses the top edge. This provides a reference point if the line gets moved inadvertently.

8

LOCATE CORNER FOOTINGS

Mark the center of the corner footings by dropping a plumb bob from a tripod (a camera tripod will do nicely) so the plumb line just touches the intersection of the layout lines. Insert a landscape spike where the plumb bob comes to rest. Tie colored tape or ribbon to the spike for visibility.

Tape marks center of footing

9

MEASURE FOOTINGS

Measure and mark the layout lines for the footing positions between the corners. Slip a small piece of tape over the line at the footing spacing.

10

MARK FOOTING CENTERS

Drop a plumb line at each piece of tape. Drive a landscape spike where the plumb bob comes to rest. Tie a piece of colored tape or ribbon to each spike for visibility. If wind disturbs the plumb line, use a piece of plywood as a windscreen.

WORK SMARTER

Equal

THE 45-DEGREE OPTION

Mark footing locations for a diagonal corner beam after creating the squared layout. Measure and mark equal distances from the intersection of the squared lines. Install batterboards with mason's line crossing the other layout lines at the marks. Drop a plumb line to locate the footings.

THE 3-4-5 TRIANGLE

The key to a precise deck layout is making the deck square. An out-of-square layout will plague you through the rest of your project — footings might end up in the wrong spots, posts and beams might be skewed, joists may end up with unequal lengths, and decking patterns might be thrown off.

Make a squared layout by establishing right angles (90 degrees) at the corners. Although a framing square forms a right angle, it is too small to accurately establish squared layout lines of the lengths needed for a deck project. But there's some simple geometry that comes to the rescue. It's known as the 3-4-5 triangle.

A triangle measuring 3 feet on one side, 4 feet on the other, with a diagonal of 5 feet will always create a perfect 90-degree angle in the corner opposite the diagonal (the hypotenuse). The same is true of multiples of 3-4-5, such as 6-8-10, 9-12-15, or 12-16-20. (Use any unit of measure with the 3-4-5 triangle, such as inches, yards, or metric units, but feet usually work best for deck layout.) Use the largest triangle your site will allow. Make reference marks at correct distances on mason's lines with marked pieces of masking tape.

TRIANGLE ESTABLISHES A SQUARE CORNER

Measure and mark 3 feet along the house or ledger from the corner you establish. (A piece of marked masking tape works well on siding.)

Measure and place a piece of marked masking tape on the mason's line (inset) so the mark is 4 feet from the corner. Place the hook end of a tape measure at the mark on the wall and measure diagonally to the mark on the string. Adjust the position of the string on the batterboard opposite the wall until this measurement is exactly 5 feet.

FREESTANDING DECK CORNER

For a freestanding deck, first set up batterboards and mason's lines. Measure and place a piece of marked tape on the first line at a multiple of 3—here we used 6 feet. Measure from the corner and place marked tape at 8 feet on the second line. The distance between the marks should be 10 feet. Move the 8-foot line to adjust as necessary.

Layout options for small decks

You don't always need to set up batterboards to lay out a deck site. Other methods might work more quickly in some situations. The decision rests largely on the size of the site. Very small installations, like concrete pads, can be laid out quite easily with a 4×8 sheet of plywood. You can lay out larger sites (up to 16 or 20 feet on a side) with either of the frame methods shown here.

Stake to firmly hold frame.

Square corners with 3-4-5 triangle.

LAYING OUT WITH 2×6s

To lay out a site with 2×6s, first make sure you have selected straight boards. Lay the boards with their inside edges representing the outside edge of the site. Use a 3-4-5 triangle (page 65) to square the boards to each other and to the house. Measure along the boards and mark the post locations on the ground. You'll need to reassemble this layout jig when you insert the J-bolts into the concrete footings.

Set string to align piers.

Outside joist

Stake to secure frame.

Header joist

FRAMING A LAYOUT

If your deck is square or rectangular, relatively small, and the yard is level, you can build the deck frame (the perimeter joists) on the ground first, use it to lay out the footings, then raise it and install it on the posts. Assemble the perimeter joists on the ground where the deck will be built. Check the corners for square with a 3-4-5 triangle and drive stakes to hold the boards firmly in place. Then mark the footing locations. Set the frame aside, pour the footings, set the posts, and cut them. Then you can either set beams and the frame on top of them or fasten the frame to the posts.

Laying out a freestanding deck

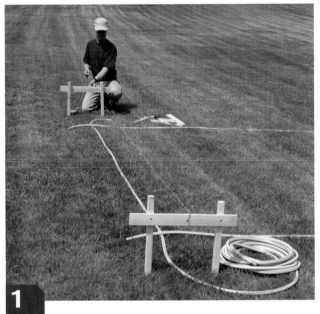

1 **MAKE ROUGH LAYOUT**

Use a garden hose to mark the approximate position for the deck. On the side of the header joist, set batterboards and string a mason's line between them to establish the centerline of the footings.

2 **SET BATTERBOARDS AT CORNERS**

Set batterboards at the next corner location and establish the centerline of the footings on this side with mason's line. Square this corner now with a 3-4-5 triangle or square the entire site after the rest of it is set.

3 **STRETCH LAYOUT LINES**

Continue setting batterboards and layout lines until all four corners are properly located. Then square each corner with a 3-4-5 triangle and measure the diagonals as extra insurance. If the diagonals are the same length, the site is square.

🌎 REAL WORLD

MEASURE TWICE, DIG ONCE

A valuable carpentry rule is: "Measure twice, cut once." Well, "Measure twice, dig once" is equally valuable for deck building. One builder didn't recheck measurements when marking the footing centers the day after setting up the basic string layout. Someone must have bumped a batterboard or stumbled into a string because a few footings ended up in the wrong places. Digging and pouring new footings was a lot of work. Save yourself backbreaking extra labor by checking the layout—at least twice!

Footings

olid, level footings establish a solid, level deck. But not just any old hole will do. Footing diameters and depths are usually prescribed by local building codes and these dimensions are the result of careful engineering science and years of experience. Codes will take into account not only the size of your proposed structure, but also local soil conditions and climate. Make sure you are designing and digging your footings according to local codes and

that you specify their dimensions on your detailed plans. Have the number, locations, and size of the footings for your deck plan approved by a building inspector before you begin to dig. It's also wise to have the local utilities mark the path of their lines. In most communities, you can get this done by calling one phone number. Use caution when digging near the marks—they're not always precise.

Chapter 4 highlights

DIGGING FOOTINGS
This is a job you can do by hand, but for anything more than four posts, you'll thank yourself for renting a power auger.

70

MIXING CONCRETE
Mixing concrete to the correct consistency is crucial to the strength of footings.

74

POURING FOOTINGS
This is another job you'll probably want to mechanize, but just in case you want to do it the old-fashioned way, we've included information about that too.

76

POURING CONCRETE PADS
Concrete pads are a different kind of footing. They support the bottom of steps and provide a base for some of the heftier amenities you might want to include in your deck.

82

Schedule an inspection of the footing holes before you pour concrete into them. The inspector will want to measure the depth before giving you the go-ahead. Schedule delivery of ready-mix concrete after you're confident your footings have passed inspection.

Digging footings

Digging footing holes by hand with a clamshell digger is quick and inexpensive, but makes sense only if you need only a few shallow holes in loamy soil. For most every other installation, you should rent a machine to make the work easier. You have two choices—either a one-person or two-person auger.

Both models dig with augers of common footing diameters (usually 8, 10, and 12 inches). You'll need a trailer hitch to tow the one-person auger home. You can forego the hitch but need a truck when renting a two-person machine.

Both machines have advantages and disadvantages. The one-person unit is counterweighted to make it easier to raise the bit out of the hole. But it's more expensive. A two-person auger is less expensive and easier to move around, but it is less powerful and you must lift the bit out of the hole yourself—no help from the machine here.

The two-person auger is useful for flaring the bottoms of holes so the footing has a larger-diameter bottom for extra stability. Otherwise you have to do it by hand.

If you hit rocks or roots, don't try to power through. Back out the auger and check to see what's obstructing the hole. Many rocks can be pried out with a pinch or pry bar. If you hit a rock ledge, check local codes to determine if you can use concrete bonding adhesive, then pour concrete on top.

When you're done digging, line the hole with a tube form and pour in a 4-inch layer of compactible gravel to assist drainage.

Two-person gas auger

One-person gas auger

Hand auger

Clamshell digger

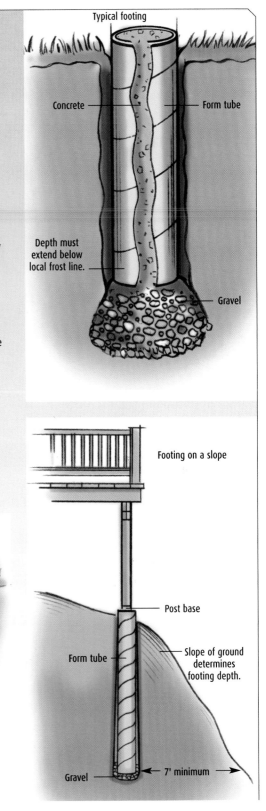

CLOSER LOOK

FOOTING REGULATIONS

Footing specifications in local building codes are based on soil conditions and the climate of the area. The depth and construction method for deck footings depends on whether the ground freezes in the winter (and the depth of the feeze, called the "frost line") and the type of soil and slope of the ground at the project site. Before digging, check with local building officials for the required hole depth and diameter. If the deck will be near a pond or marshy area, footings may need to be larger than normal to adequately support the deck.

A typical footing (top right) is a round hole filled with concrete. The footing must be deep enough to be below the frost line in cold climates. That's because freezing and thawing cycles cause the ground to heave above the frost line. This movement can shift portions of the deck structure and cause major structural problems. Extending footings below the frost line prevents this damage. You also may be required to flare the bottom of the hole. Making the footing bottom wider than the top prevents movement of the footing in the ground. A layer of compactible gravel (usually 3–6 inches thick) is frequently required in the bottom of the hole to drain water away from the base of the footing. Tube forms may be required by codes in your area, especially in loose soils. Even if they aren't required, they are a good addition to a footing hole. If nothing else, the tubes prevent the hole from collapsing before concrete is poured. They also keep moisture in the concrete from being absorbed too quickly by the surrounding soil, which weakens the concrete.

Footings in areas where the soil doesn't freeze (bottom left) are often square and shallow (2×2 feet and 1 foot deep are common). This type of footing usually doesn't require a separate form. If one is necessary, cover the sides of the hole with pieces of treated plywood. Some areas don't require in-ground footings—precast concrete piers can be set directly on level ground (page 81).

On sloping ground, the bottom of the footing must be "7 feet from daylight" at the incline (bottom right). On steep slopes, this means deep holes. When working on a steep slope, hire a professional to install footings and frame the deck.

4

FOOTINGS

Typical footing

Concrete — — Form tube

Depth must
extend below
local frost line.

— Gravel

Footing on a slope

Post base

Form tube —

Slope of ground
determines
footing depth.

Gravel — 7' minimum

Frost-free footing

Concrete poured
into excavation
without forms

— Gravel

4

FOOTINGS

1

BORE THE FOOTING HOLE

Remove the layout lines and the spike marking the center of the footing. Start the hole with the bit extension that will keep the handles about waist high. Rock the tool slightly as its auger turns. When you reach the proper depth, rock the auger with the bit at the bottom of the hole to flare the base of the footing.

2

TAMP IN GRAVEL

Remove any loose soil either by hand or with a clamshell digger and tamp a layer of compactible gravel to the code-required thickness (usually 3–6 inches). Use a post, a tamper, or pinch bar to compact the gravel.

3

SET THE FORM TUBE

Install a footing base in the bottom of the hole and cut the tube form to length. Level the top of the form so the footing will be level when you pour it.

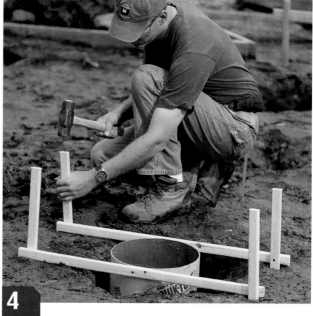

4

BRACE THE TUBE

Brace the tube in place to make certain it stays level. If the form shifts slightly from center, don't worry. You just need to make sure the post base is centered when you make the pour.

5 BACKFILL AROUND TUBE

Backfill around the form but don't tamp the dirt too much. This may distort the shape or shift the position of the form. If the footing hole is significantly larger than the form, wait to backfill until you've poured the concrete. Otherwise dirt will fill the flared portion of the hole.

WORK SMARTER

USE FORMS FOR A GROUND-LEVEL DECK

Use forms even if they're not required by local code. They are the easiest way to make footings with tops that are level with each other. Pour concrete as for other footings (see the following pages). Set batterboards so the crosspieces are level with each other and about 1 inch above grade.

TOOL SAVVY

DIGGING WITH A CLAMSHELL DIGGER

A clamshell digger is handy even if you dig footing holes with a gas-powered auger. Use it to remove loose dirt that an auger can't lift from the bottom of a hole. The clamshell digger also can be used to flare a footing hole, and it's an option when you have only a few shallow holes to dig.

Here's how to use it. Push the handles together (top right) to spread the blades before ramming it into the dirt. Pull the handles apart (center), forcing the blades together to capture loose dirt. Keep the handles spread to bring dirt out of the hole. Open the blades to dump the dirt. Pile dirt removed from footing holes on plastic sheeting when working on grass to make it easier to haul away without damaging the grass. Don't leave the loaded plastic down too long in hot weather—the grass under it may wilt within a day.

Mixing concrete

PROJECT DETAILS

SKILLS: Mixing with a shovel
PROJECT: Mixing two bags of concrete by hand

TIME TO COMPLETE

EXPERIENCED: *
HANDY: 7 min.
NOVICE: 10 min.
*Generally, experienced builders don't mix by hand.

STUFF YOU'LL NEED

TOOLS: Wheelbarrow, shovel, trowel
MATERIALS: Premix concrete, drinkable water

There are a number of ways to get concrete into your footings. You can mix it in a wheelbarrow from premixed bags, you can mix it from dry ingredients in a power mixer, or you can call in the ready-mix truck. The decision is largely a matter of how much concrete you have to pour, and whether you want to devote effort or devote money to the task. To help you decide, start with an accurate estimate of how much concrete you will need (see page 25). If you have more than a cubic yard to pour, it's best to hire the ready-mix pros.

Concrete is caustic; use caution when working with it. Wear eye protection, a dust mask, and long clothing. Avoid dropping bags of cement and creating dust clouds.

Concrete must be mixed to the correct consistency for strength and durability. A runny mix means you've added too much water. Pour in more premix if there is room in the wheelbarrow. Combine the new ingredients thoroughly with the runny batch before adding more water—it may not be needed. Test the mix as necessary until the batch reaches the proper consistency.

Test the mix by scooping up some on a trowel. A mix of the proper consistency holds its shape, and no water is visible. Continue adding increasingly smaller amounts of water and mixing until the consistency is just right.

MIX CONCRETE IN A LARGE WHEELBARROW
Empty a bag of premix concrete into the wheelbarrow. (Never use a partial bag of premix concrete because it won't have the correct proportion of ingredients.) With a shovel, make a depression in the mound of premix and pour about one-half gallon of clean water into it. Begin mixing by moving dry material from the sides of the mound into the water-filled depression. Work carefully so you don't slop water out of the wheelbarrow, which will remove some of the ingredients necessary for a proper mix.

TOOL SAVVY

POWER MIXING SAVES TIME AND MUSCLES

Mixing concrete in a wheelbarrow is fine when you only have a few shallow footings to fill. Each 60-lb. bag of premix concrete makes ½ cubic foot of concrete—enough to fill about 6 inches of a 12 inch-diameter tube form. Rent a power mixer to make your work much easier if you have more than a dozen bags to mix. The type shown here is portable; the concrete can be mixed and poured at each footing location.

Make sure you understand how to operate the power mixer safely before leaving the rental center. (An electric power mixer should be plugged into a GFCI-protected outlet or extension cord.) Never reach hands or tools into the mixer while it is operating. Stop the mixer to check the mix consistency.

Mix each batch of concrete to the proper consistency. Each batch will take a few minutes. After dumping the previous batch, pour about one-third of the premix and one-half the water for the next batch into the mixer. Run it for a minute to gather residue from the previous batch before adding the remaining materials and finishing the new batch.

WORK SMARTER

THE SIMPLEST MIXING METHOD

For a large number of footings, have ready-mix concrete delivered by a commercial concrete supplier. Specify that the concrete will be used for deck footings and how much you need (page 25). The contractor will provide the proper concrete mix to your site. (Many suppliers set a minimum purchase.) Make sure you have the holes approved by the inspector before scheduling the concrete delivery. The ready-mix driver will want to dump the load quickly. Ask when you order the concrete how much time you'll have to unload from the time the truck arrives. The driver will not help you unload or fill holes, so have some friends with wheelbarrows ready to carry the concrete from the truck and dump it into the footing holes. Most concrete companies also provide the option of pumping the concrete from the delivery truck through a hose (above) directly to the holes. The ease and time savings of this option are usually well worth any extra cost.

Pouring footings

REAL WORLD

KEEP THE BATTERBOARDS
It's a good idea to leave the batterboards in place until after you pour the footings. If you accidently dislodge a reference spike or otherwise lose a center mark, it's easy to retie the mason's string lines at the marks on the crosspieces. Then you can accurately reset the centers without wasting much time.

No matter what method you use to pour your footings, pouring them involves more than just dumping concrete in. There are several things you must do to the concrete after it's in the footing and before it hardens.

First move your wheelbarrow or mixer as close to the footing as you can before mixing the concrete.

Second always pour a complete footing. If you need to mix another batch of concrete to finish filling a hole, do so before the first batch dries. Pouring fresh concrete over dry concrete creates a so-called cold joint in the hole where the new concrete won't adhere to the old. This situation will compromise the footing strength.

Once the concrete is in the footing, you'll have to screed (level) it. If you're pouring a pad, you'll have to float it, edge it, and finish it.

After the concrete is poured, you can install an anchor for a post base, using one of three methods: Push a J-bolt into the wet concrete, place a wet-insert post base, or let the concrete cure and drill a hole for a threaded stud.

1 **USE A SHOVEL**
Guide concrete into the footing hole with a shovel. This type of power mixer allows you to mix at the footing and pour directly from the mixer into the hole. You also can pour from a wheelbarrow, but it's better to use a round-nosed shovel and scoop the concrete from the wheelbarrow. Some concrete may slop outside the form, but don't scrape it up and put it into the footing—dirt weakens the mix.

2   PUDDLE THE CONCRETE

Plunge a length of scrap wood into the concrete when the footing is almost full. Work it up and down to eliminate air pockets. On footings deeper than 2 feet, do this when the footing is half full and again when completely full.

3   SCREED THE SURFACE

Remove excess concrete with a length of 2×4 and level the top of the footing after overfilling the form slightly. Push the 2×4 back and forth in a sawing motion as you pull it across the tube form.

CLOSER LOOK

REINFORCE FOOTINGS

Local codes may require reinforcing footings with rebar. This is common on footing columns that are several feet above ground level. Cut pieces of rebar about 4 inches shorter than the depth of the footing. Insert the rebar into wet concrete after screeding the surface. Each piece should be at least 2 inches from the sides of the tube form with its top end at least 3 inches below the concrete surface. Add concrete and smooth as necessary.

4   INSERT THE J-BOLT

Either reset the layout lines or use a story pole to mark the center of the footings. Insert the hooked end of a J-bolt into the wet concrete at the center of the footing. (The J-bolt can be off just a little—you'll position the post base precisely because it's adjustable.) Leave 1 inch of the threads showing above the surface of the concrete.

4

5 **SQUARE THE J-BOLT**

Square the J-bolt to the footing. Add concrete and smooth as necessary. Let the concrete cure for about 48 hours. In hot weather, especially in direct sun, mist the concrete occasionally so it doesn't cure too quickly, which may make it brittle. If it is hot, cover the footings with clear plastic sheeting after misting.

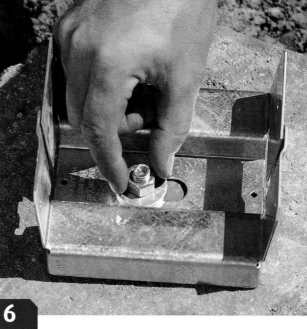

6 **INSTALL THE POST BASE**

Set an adjustable post base over the threads of the J-bolt and tighten each nut so the base can still be adjusted.

7 **ALIGN POST BASES**

Line up the post bases parallel to the house by setting a straight 2×4 or other long straightedge across the footings and against the flanges of the post bases. Measure from the house to the edge of the 2×4 and adjust the post bases till they are equidistant from the rear wall. Mark each base position on its footing with a pencil. These marks will help you gauge anchor position adjustments as well as provide a reference point if a post base is knocked out of alignment. Then line up the post bases on the sides of the site, restringing the layout lines if necessary to keep the bases in the same plane.

8

CHECK THE DIAGONALS
Measure the diagonals after aligning all the post anchors. Make adjustments as necessary until the measurements are equal. (You may have to readjust the other post bases too.) This makes the post positions square to each other and to the house.

9

TIGHTEN POST BASE NUT
Tighten each nut with a socket wrench to secure the post bases. The anchor should not move, and do not overtighten the nut.

Installing a wet-insert post base

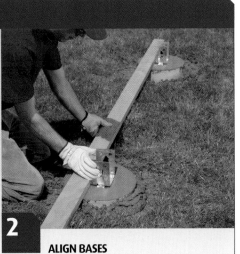

1

PUSH BASE INTO WET CONCRETE
Insert the fins of a wet-insert post base (also known as a finned base) into wet, screeded concrete. Use a story pole to position the base accurately in the footing. Rock the base slightly as you push the fins into the concrete. This type of base is required by some local building codes.

2

ALIGN BASES
Use a long straightedge (or story pole) to align post bases to each other—or restring the layout lines to keep them centered. Work with a helper if you have several footings. This type of post base is more difficult to install because of the extra alignment necessary while the concrete is still wet. Let the concrete cure (see Step 5, opposite page).

📖 WORK SMARTER

LINE 'EM UP
You must be accurate when placing wet-insert bases because they can't be moved once the concrete cures. Place a board alongside the bases to make sure they line up before the concrete sets.

Installing threaded studs

1

DRILL THE FOOTING

Drill a hole for a threaded stud that will hold the post base to each footing. Use a hammer drill and a masonry bit of the same diameter as the threaded stud. Set the depth gauge on the drill so ¾ to 1 inch of the threads will remain above the footing surface. Locate each hole position with a story pole or restring the mason's lines to mark the center of the footings. Use a layout square to keep the drill bit vertical.

2

CLEAN OUT THE HOLE

Remove drilling debris with a shop vacuum. Clean the hole thoroughly so the epoxy used to secure the stud will firmly bond with the concrete.

3

INJECT EPOXY

Inject structural epoxy into the hole with the mixing syringe provided by the manufacturer. Fill the hole about halfway with epoxy, then insert a threaded stud—the epoxy begins to harden immediately. Wrap a piece of masking tape around the top threads to indicate the proper depth. If a small amount of epoxy pushes from the hole when you insert the stud, you've injected the right amount. You can remove the stud and inject more epoxy if you work quickly. One syringe contains enough epoxy for four to six holes. Wipe excess epoxy with a rag. Wear gloves when using epoxy.

4

POSITION STUD

Check the height of the stud above the footing, making sure that about 1 inch of thread is showing. Let the epoxy cure for 16 to 24 hours. Follow the manufacturer's directions—curing times vary according to temperature and moisture conditions.

4

FOOTINGS

Precast concrete piers

Precast concrete piers can sometimes be used instead of deep footings depending on ground conditions, the type of deck, and the requirements of local codes.

When they are used with footings, the footings are usually square and level with the ground. The square recesses in the piers support posts. The rectangular grooves support 2× lumber (such as rim joists) on edge.

1
WET PRECAST PIERS

Soak precast concrete piers in water before inserting them into a wet concrete footing. Dry piers draw moisture away from the concrete in the footing and weaken the bond. Pour the footing while the piers are soaking.

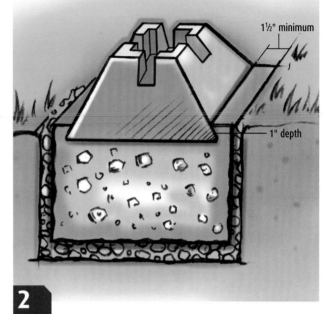

1½" minimum

1" depth

2
ALIGN PIERS ON FOOTINGS

Align the pier on the footing after screeding the concrete surface. The footing should be at least 1½ inches wider than the pier on each side. Push the pier about 1 inch into the concrete. Make certain the top of the pier remains level. Smooth the footing surface and let the concrete cure (see page 78). Bolt a metal post base to the pier (below) for a raised deck.

 REAL WORLD

DON'T TRUST HISTORY
Friends and neighbors who have built decks will offer you a lot of advice. Some of it will be helpful, but double-check anything that involves building codes. One builder followed his neighbor's advice about footings because the building inspector had approved the neighbor's deck a few years before. But local code regulations had changed since that deck was built. The builder muttered, "Get plan approval first, then dig," all the while as he broke out the old footings and dug new ones.

PRECAST CONCRETE PIER OPTION:
Precast piers also can be used when footings aren't required by local code. The pier is placed directly on level, firm ground (though code may require a layer of compactible gravel underneath it). Bolt a metal post base to the pier (page 40) even if not required by local code; the base securely fastens a post to the pier.

4

FOOTINGS

Pouring concrete pads

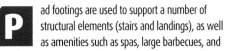

PROJECT DETAILS

SKILLS: Measuring, digging, cutting and fastening lumber; mixing; pouring; screeding; and finishing concrete
PROJECT: Marking, digging, pouring, and screeding a 4×4-foot pad

TIME TO COMPLETE

EXPERIENCED: 5 hrs.
HANDY: 7 hrs.
NOVICE: 8 hrs.

STUFF YOU'LL NEED

TOOLS: Tape measure, shovel, tamper, reciprocating saw, drill, hammer, level, power mixer, masonry finishing tools
MATERIALS: Lumber, compactible gravel, premix concrete, 3-mil plastic sheeting

Pad footings are used to support a number of structural elements (stairs and landings), as well as amenities such as spas, large barbecues, and hot tubs. In most cases pad footings are square or rectangular, which makes their layout relatively easy. You can use batterboards and mason's lines as if you were laying out a deck site (the method shown on the following pages), or for smaller projects you can use a sheet of plywood, 2×6 boards, or deck framing (see page 66).

Ground-level pads are usually built to support stairs. Raised pads are often employed to support heavy amenities incorporated into the deck design (a raised spa on a deck platform, for example)

In all cases, make the pad at least 3 inches wider on each side than the base of the item it supports. The thickness of the pad and any reinforcing material required will be a matter determined by local codes. Four inches of concrete over a 4-inch gravel bed is common, but don't assume those specifications will pass inspection everywhere. Take your plans to the building department before you start digging.

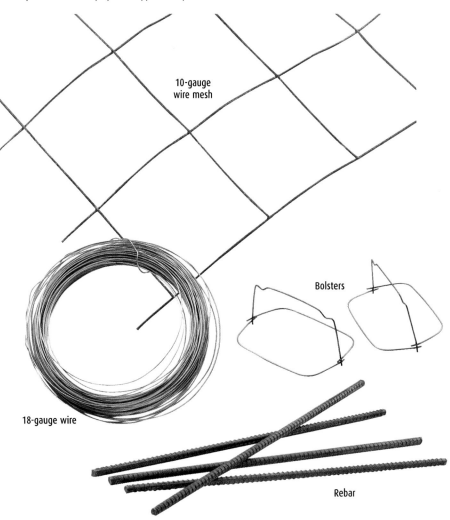

10-gauge wire mesh

Bolsters

18-gauge wire

Rebar

CONCRETE REINFORCEMENT

Special reinforcing materials are often required by local codes for poured pad footings. For large concrete pads, 10-gauge wire mesh is often used. It comes in flat sections, often 3 feet by 3 feet, or in long rolls that are 4 feet wide. Cut it to size with heavy side cutters or a bolt cutter. Rebar is a steel reinforcing bar also known as reinforcing rod. Pieces of rebar are fastened together in a grid for pads (or used individually in column footings). Fasten pieces of mesh or rebar together with 18-gauge wire. Bolsters help keep the wire mesh centered in the thickness of the concrete.

Pouring a ground-level pad

1 **LAY OUT THE SITE**

Lay out the site with batterboards and mason's lines using the techniques for laying out a deck (pages 62–67). Outline the perimeter of the pad with chalk or marking paint. Remove the sod and excavate the site, then build 2×4 forms anchored firmly with stakes. Square the form by measuring the diagonals and adjusting it as necessary until they are equal. Make sure the form is level on all four sides.

 **DESIGN TIP**

ALTERNATE LANDINGS

Concrete is not the only material you can choose for stair landings. Brick and precast pavers make an excellent landing surface and bring a stylish design element to your deck site. Installation of a brick landing is similar to that of a concrete pad. It involves layout and excavation, then depending on local codes, setting the paving over a mortared surface or sand bed.

TOOL SAVVY

CONCRETE TOOLS FINISH THE JOB

Inexpensive concrete tools will contribute to a professional-looking concrete pad. A pointing trowel is used to separate the concrete from the form. (It also is handy to test proper consistency of the concrete mix.) A margin trowel is a general-purpose trowel used in small areas or corners. A float creates a smooth surface on concrete. A metal float makes a hard, smooth finish. Texture the surface of a stair pad with a stiff driveway broom to provide safe traction if you use a metal float. A wood float leaves a slightly rougher surface than the metal float. Use an edger to round the edges of a pad so they won't chip as easily as square edges.

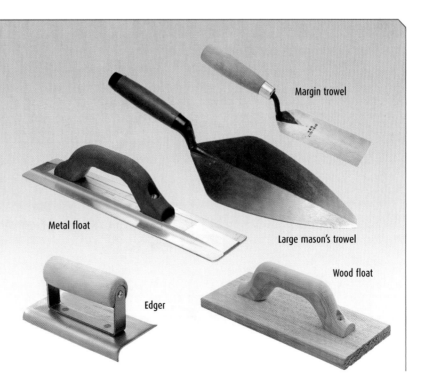

Margin trowel

Metal float

Large mason's trowel

Wood float

Edger

Pouring a ground-level pad *(continued)*

WORK SMARTER

CUTTING REBAR

Rebar is tough stuff—if you have a lot of pieces to cut with a hacksaw, it will wear out your arm. Use a metal-cutting blade in a reciprocating saw. Clamp the rebar to a piece of wood and keep the saw foot against the rebar while cutting.

2 TAMP THE GRAVEL BASE

Tamp a layer of compactible gravel of the code-required thickness over the ground. Make this as level as possible so the correct thickness of concrete can be poured. Position reinforcement (page 82) over the gravel if required (local code didn't require reinforcement for this pad). Coat the inside of the form with vegetable oil or form-release agent for easy form removal.

3 FILL THE FORMS, THEN SCREED

Mix the concrete and shovel it into the forms. Run a 2×4 up and down in the mix, then screed the surface with a 2×4 . Fill low spots with more concrete and screed again if necessary.

4 FLOAT THE SURFACE

Smooth, or float, the concrete surface with a float. Float the concrete just long enough to make it smooth and to bring a thin layer of water (bleed water) to the surface. Finish floating quickly after bleed water appears.

5 FREE THE FORM

Push the point of a small trowel into the concrete at the form. Slide the trowel along the edge of the pad to help free the form from the concrete.

6

EDGE THE PAD

Work an edger around the perimeter seam to smooth and round off the edges of the pad (round edges won't chip as easily as square ones). Work the edger in both directions, raising the leading edge slightly so it doesn't dig into the concrete.

7

TEXTURE THE SURFACE

Roughen the pad surface with a stiff bristle broom. The texture increases traction for pads at the foot of stairs. Cover the pad and let the concrete cure for a week.

Pouring a raised pad

Construction of a raised pad proceeds in the same order as a ground-level pad. The two major differences are the additional bracing required and filling the form with rubble as shown at right.

BRACE THE FORMS

Cut cleats and fasten them to the tops of each corner. Brace the cleats from below with stakes and braces. Place one end of a brace under a cleat and drive a 1-foot-long 1×3 stake into the ground at the foot of the brace to wedge it in place.

REINFORCE THE PAD

Fill the forms to at least one-third of their depth with clean rubble (broken chunks of concrete make good filler material). Place the reinforcement (10-gauge wire mesh for this project) within the thickness of the concrete but no closer than 4 inches to the sides of the form.

Framing

raming starts to bring a little more excitement to your project. It's when the frame starts to go up that the contours of the deck begin to appear, and you can see the results of your design, planning, and effort begin to take shape.

Framing is the support structure for the deck, the base for the more aesthetic aspects of your deck. Framing consists of posts, beams, and joists. The framing itself can greatly affect the appearance of your deck,

even if you use lumber that's less expensive than you employ on the decking and railing. That's why you should pay close attention to making square corners and clean, straight cuts. Drive fasteners flush with the surface of the wood for best appearance.

Attention to all of these details not only creates a support structure that contributes to, rather than detracts from, the overall appearance of the deck, it also ensures that the deck won't fall down.

Chapter 5 highlights

SETTING AND CUTTING POSTS
This is where the fun begins. You can see the outlines and the shape of your deck start to take form.

88

NOTCHING A POST
Notches provide a nice aesthetic alternative to a few other fastening methods.

90

BUILDING AND INSTALLING BEAMS
Beams are the workhorses of deck construction, and different kinds of decks will call for different beam configurations.

93

INSTALLING JOISTS
Joists support the decking and must be laid straight and fastened solidly to the perimeter frame.

98

BLOCKING THE JOISTS
These short lengths of lumber add a whole lot of stability to the joists.

103

INSTALLING JOISTS AROUND OBSTRUCTIONS
Rather than work against nature, it saves time and money to work with it by incorporating trees and other obstacles right into your deck design.

104

Because framing lumber is heavy, it's wise to enlist the aid of a helper or two. You can do the work by yourself, but a joint effort makes the project more enjoyable and easier on your body.

Don't scrimp on fasteners. An adage in the construction business says that when a structure fails, it's the fasteners that go first. Use fasteners specified by the manufacturer for framing connectors. The strength and holding power of metal connectors depends on the correct fasteners.

Setting and cutting posts

Posts must be plumb for your deck to be stable and so other framing members can be accurately aligned. Setting posts is ideally a two-person job. There's a lot of precise work required here, and additional hands and eyes will help immensely. The easiest method for cutting posts to length is to do so after installing them in post anchors.

1

CHECK THE POST ENDS

Check the ends of each post with a layout square. If neither end is square, mark and square one end and use that end in the post base. You're going to cut the other end to the proper height later, so it doesn't matter if it's not square. The post should be as straight as possible and longer than needed so you can trim it to length after attaching it to the footing.

WORK SMARTER

GIVE IT A QUICK DIP

Coat freshly cut surfaces on pressure-treated lumber with preservative. The pressure treatment isn't always absorbed completely through the wood, especially in 4× and larger lumber. Dipping cut ends in a bucket containing preservative is simple. Brush preservative on surfaces cut in place, such as notches.

2

TACK THE POST IN PLACE

Set the square end of the post in the post base and drive one nail halfway into the center hole of one of the post-base flanges. This will keep the post in the base and allow enough movement so you can plumb it. Drive the nail only halfway so you can reposition it if necessary.

3

BRACE THE POST

Stake 1×4 braces to the ground and tack them to the post with partially driven screws. Strap a post level on the post at a place where you can see the vials in the level while you plumb the post and fasten the braces securely. Install, brace, and plumb the remaining posts in the same way.

4

RECHECK THE LAYOUT

Restring the layout lines to make sure the faces of the posts all lie in the same plane. Then drive a nail into each hole in the post-base flanges.

5

MARK THE POST HEIGHT

Mark the posts for the cut line either level with the bottom of the ledger or below this level by the depth of the joists and beam, depending on your construction method. Measure down from this mark the width of the beam if the joists will be supported by a beam.

6

DRAW CUTTING LINES

Using a layout square, extend the cut line around the post. Make the mark with a carpenter's pencil—dark enough so you can see it when the saw kicks up the sawdust.

7

SAW THE POST

Holding a reciprocating saw securely, position the shoe against one corner (angle the saw against the corner) with the blade lined up with, but not touching, the cut line. Start the saw and tilt the blade into the cut line, keeping it level throughout the cut.

Notching a post

PROJECT DETAILS

SKILLS: Measuring and layout, cutting lumber, smoothing with a chisel
PROJECT: Notching one post, working alone

TIME TO COMPLETE

EXPERIENCED: 10 min.
HANDY: 15 min.
NOVICE: 20 min.

STUFF YOU'LL NEED

TOOLS: Tape measure, layout square, circular saw, hammer, chisel
MATERIALS: Lumber

Cutting a center notch

1 MAKE THE NOTCH SHOULDERS

If your footings are all exactly level with each other, use pipe clamps to hold several posts together and mark the edges of the notches on all the posts at the same time. Cut the edges of the notch with a circular saw whose blade depth is set equal to the depth of the notch. If you're only cutting one notch, guide the saw with a layout square so these shoulder cuts are straight and square.

2 CUT THE KERFS

Make multiple cuts with the circular saw between the shoulder cuts. A layout square isn't necessary here because these cuts don't need to be square. The object is to make enough kerfs to leave thin sections that you can remove with a hammer and chisel.

3 CLEAN OUT THE NOTCH

Break out the waste sections with a hammer. Be careful not to mar the ends of the notch.

4 SQUARE THE NOTCH WITH A CHISEL

Cut the remaining waste material from the bottom of the notch with a sharp 1-inch chisel. Cut with the beveled edge of the chisel facing up.

Notching across a post end

SAW A NOTCH ON TOP
Cut down the shoulder line of the notch on the top of a post with a reciprocating saw. Then crosscut the perpendicular line and remove the waste piece.

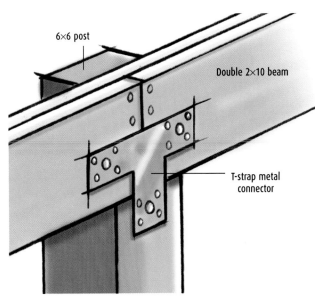

6×6 post

Double 2×10 beam

T-strap metal connector

NOTCH THE POST FOR A BEAM
Cut a notch across the end of a post when it will hold a beam. This is an alternative to installing the beam on top of the post. Some local codes require an additional metal framing connector to tie the beam to the notched post.

Cutting an inside corner notch

1

SAW-CUT THE SHOULDERS
Begin the first long shoulder cut with a circular saw set to the depth of the notch. Stop cutting with the saw just before you reach the corners. If you have trouble balancing the saw on the edge of the post, slip another post next to the one you're working on to give the saw a little more base support.

2

STOP AT THE LINE
Stop the saw when the blade reaches the end of the notch. Cut through at the top of the notch using a sharp chisel. Use the chisel to clean out the corner and faces of the notch and to make it square.

Cutting an outside corner notch

CUT THE SHOULDERS
Use a circular saw to make the long shoulder cuts. Stop the saw blade just before you reach the corners.

FINISH WITH A RECIPROCATING SAW
Use a reciprocating saw with a woodcutting blade to complete the cuts, if necessary. Use a chisel to finish out the corners.

REAL WORLD

MEASURE EACH POST
Timesaving ideas can cost time if you're not careful. Faced with cutting notches in a dozen posts, a builder marked and cut the notch for one, then used that post to mark the next one. That post was cut, then was used as a template to mark the next one and so on until all the posts were notched. After the last cut, the builder discovered that the notch location was ¼ inch off between the first and last posts! Some of the cuts weren't accurate and using each newly cut post to mark the next increased the error. Measuring and marking each post would have been quicker in the long run.

DESIGN TIP

SECURE BOARDS IN NOTCHES
Attaching beams and rim joists to posts by securing them in notches is an alternative to using metal framing connectors. Many local codes allow this method. You may think the deck is more attractive without the metal and you'll save the cost of connectors. However, cutting notches is more difficult and takes more time than using connectors. Check local codes—some codes allow notching but require an additional metal connector.

5

FRAMING

Building and installing beams

THE BASIC BEAMS

The three basic beam types: (**A**) Two pieces of 2× lumber sandwiched around posts. Although allowed by building code, this type of beam is not as strong as the others. (**B**) A solid, large piece of lumber (4×6 minimum) attached to post tops. (**C**) Two or more pieces of 2× lumber fastened together to form a beam attached to post tops.

Most beams are not made of solid lumber but of lengths of 2× stock fastened together. That's because solid 4×6 (and larger) lumber long enough for beams is difficult to find, more expensive than an equivalent beam built from 2× stock, and more susceptible to warping or twisting.

When building beams, you have a number of options. The steps that start at right show how to build a beam from 2×10 lumber before raising it into position. Making a beam from 2×12 lumber attached to two faces of the posts is shown on page 95. Before you use this style of beam, make sure your local building codes allow it, because it is the weakest of the options.

Installing beams on top of posts

1

JOIN THE BOARDS
Clamp the boards together crown side up on a sturdy work surface. Drive three 3-inch galvanized deck screws (at a slight angle) at each end of the board and every 12 inches. Screws should be no closer than 1½ inches to the board edges.

2

SET THE BEAM ON THE POSTS
Raise the beam and set it in place on top of the posts. You can either fasten the beam to the posts with toenailed screws or attach it with post caps.

Installing beams on top of posts *(continued)*

3 ATTACH THE BEAM

Level the beam with cedar shims, if necessary. Drive a nail of the type specified by the manufacturer through each hole in the post cap flanges. Center a beam joint on the center of the post and strengthen the joints with a T-strap if required by code.

4 REINFORCE THE CORNER

Attach an angle bracket to reinforce the corners, using as large a bracket as the corner will allow. Use nails specified by the bracket manufacturer.

5 PROTECT THE TOP OF THE BEAM

Protect the joint along the beam with caulking or apply self-sealing waterproofing membrane over the top of the beam. Cut a strip of membrane about 6 inches wide. Roll it up with the paper backing facing out. Starting at one end of the beam, press the self-adhesive surface onto the beam, pulling the paper off as you go.

CLOSER LOOK

BEAMS WITH OVERLAPPING ENDS

When making beams with overlapping ends, build the beam so its outside face is 1½ inches longer than its inside face. Set the beam in place on the posts and fasten it to post cap connectors. Fit the rim joist into the spaces at the end of the beams.

WORK SMARTER

FILL THE GAP

A beam made of two pieces of 2× lumber will leave a ½-inch gap when placed in a nonadjustable post cap for 4×4 posts. Fill this gap with a shim made from ½-inch pressure-treated plywood. Cut the shim so it extends 2 inches beyond the post cap flanges. Caulk the seams around the shim with silicone caulk. Place the shim on the side where it will be least visible.

Sandwiching a beam around posts

1

MARK THE BEAM HEIGHT

Use a water level to mark the height of the beam on the corner posts. Then snap a chalk line between the posts to mark all the posts at the same height. Extend the line around the posts to the opposite side with a layout square.

2

ATTACH BEAM BOARDS

Attach the inner board on the chalk line with two screws at each post. The ends of the inner beam should be flush with post edges. If you need more than one board for a long beam, center the joint on the post. Attach the outer board similarly. Make the outer beam board 1½ inches longer than the inner beam board at each end if a rim joist will be installed on the same plane.

3

DRILL BOLT HOLES

Drill holes through both beam boards and the post for two ½-inch carriage bolts. Stagger the holes on either side of the center of the post to prevent splitting. Attach metal connectors if required by local code.

4

INSTALL BOLTS

Insert carriage bolts from the outside face of the beam and slip a washer over the threads. Thread a nut on each carriage bolt and tighten it with a socket wrench. Tighten each nut until the washer begins to sink into the wood.

Installing diagonal beams

 nstall a beam at a 45-degree angle when your plan calls for an alternative decking pattern that requires diagonal support.

🔍 **CLOSER LOOK**

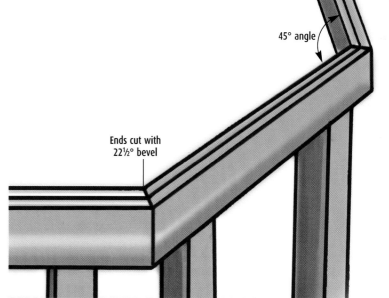

45° angle

Ends cut with 22½° bevel

DIAGONAL PERIMETER BEAM

Some deck designs require that a beam be installed at 45 degrees on the perimeter of the deck. The framing that the 45-degree beam attaches to should be installed first. Cut boards for the 45-degree beam longer than needed. Clamp them together and mark the length. Cut the ends of the 45-degree beam and the framing to which it attaches at 22½-degree angles.

1 POSITION BEAM TO MARK LENGTH

Mark the point where each side of the diagonal beam will intersect the existing framing at the corner. Clamp the boards together and set them on the existing framing to mark beam length accurately. Unclamp the boards, then cut them to length with a circular saw set at 45 degrees.

2 FASTEN BEAM

Install the sections of the beam one at a time. Hold one diagonal section in place and predrill for the fasteners. Drive screws into the beam through the existing frame. Install the second section in the same fashion.

3 REINFORCE CORNERS

Attach a skewable angle bracket to reinforce the corners on each side of the beam. Use as large a bracket as the corner will allow.

Post supports beam

FRAMING

5

Installing beams on footings

1 **ATTACH THE BEAM**
Attach the beam to the post bases with each end extending no farther than 1 foot beyond a footing. Build the beam with the inside faces 1½ inches shorter than the outer face at each end, or build a solid beam with flush edges. Insert a ½-inch shim between the beam and the post base as shown on page 94.

2 **CHECK FOR SQUARE**
Measure the diagonals between the beam ends. Adjust the post anchor and beam positions until the measurements are equal and the deck is square. Install joists as shown on pages 98–102.

Make sure the concrete has time to cure.

Post bracing

Local codes may require permanent bracing of deck posts. This is most common on attached decks more than 8 feet high and freestanding decks more than 3 feet high. The size and number of posts also affects whether or not bracing is required. Posts supporting a small raised stair landing often require permanent bracing also. Attach bracing before installing joists.

LEAVE A GAP
Cut brace sections so the cut ends are vertical when installed. Leave a ⅛- to ¼-inch gap between the ends to prevent trapping moisture. Deck screws hold the bracing before you drill holes and install permanent fasteners.

PUT BLOCK AT CROSSOVER
Attach a short piece of post between crossed bracing members for stability. The piece should be at least 9 inches long to prevent splitting. Fasten it with lag screws or a carriage bolt.

Installing joists

J oists support the decking. Install them with 12-, 16-, or 24-inch spacing between their centers, depending on the thickness of decking material, the installation pattern of the decking, and local building codes. Choose quality lumber that is as straight as possible. Install each joist with its crown side up. Attach joists to framing with metal joist hangers. The joists on this project are 15 feet long, installed 16 inches on center, and sit on top of the beam. They are cantilevered about 2 feet beyond the beam.

1

INSTALL RIM JOISTS

Cut the rim joists to the proper length and attach one end to the end of the ledger with 3-inch deck screws. The opposite end of the rim joist will be supported by the beam.

2

ATTACH RIM JOISTS TO BEAM

Set the outer edge of the rim joist flush with the end of the beam and toenail the joist temporarily with a 3-inch screw. Fasten the other rim joist with the same procedures.

3

INSTALL HEADER JOIST

Fasten the header joist to the ends of the rim joists with 3-inch predrilled deck screws spaced 2 to 3 inches apart.

4 ADD SEISMIC TIES

Fasten the rim joists permanently to the beam with seismic/hurricane ties. Use nails specified by the connector manufacturer.

5 REINFORCE THE CORNERS

Attach an angle bracket in each corner of the joist frame to reinforce the joint. Use as long a bracket as the lumber size allows.

6 INSTALL A JOIST HANGER

Mark the joist locations on the ledger and header and measure the width of the joist. Attach one side of a joist hanger at the first location. Place it so the joist will rest on the bottom of the flange and lie flush with the top edges of the header and ledger.

7 PLACE THE JOIST

Set the joist in the hanger and fasten the other side of the hanger, making sure it's snug against the joists. Then drive a nail through every nail hole in the hanger—the strength of the hanger connection depends on proper nailing.

8 INSTALL REMAINING JOISTS

Install the remaining joists. Measure the joist length at each location for best results. Attach each joist hanger based on the actual width of the board it will hold.

Installing joists on a diagonal corner

PROJECT DETAILS

SKILLS: Measuring and marking angles, cutting lumber, driving fasteners
PROJECT: Installing joists at a 45-degree angle at a deck corner

TIME TO COMPLETE

EXPERIENCED: 20 min.
HANDY: 40 min.
NOVICE: 1 hr.

STUFF YOU'LL NEED

TOOLS: Tape measure, chalk line, layout square, circular saw, drill, hammer
MATERIALS: Lumber, fasteners

5

FRAMING

All corners on a deck do not necessarily have to be 90-degree intersections. Some installations will call for a diagonal header for stylistic reasons or to conform to conditions of the landscape or the walls of the house. Diagonal corners are easy to construct, with a few extra steps and diagonal joist hangers. In this installation the joists are installed on top of the beams.

1

BRACE JOISTS FOR CUTTING

Install the joists using joist hangers, but do not fasten those joists that will be cut on the diagonal. Make sure the header and rim joist are long enough to extend beyond the intersection of the diagonal. Attach temporary braces across the last several joists to keep them in place.

2 **MARK DIAGONAL**
Mark the header and rim joist at the intersection of the diagonal and snap a chalk line between the marks across the joists.

45° angle on interior joists

22½° angle on header and rim joists

5

WORK SMARTER

HANGING 45s

Attach one side of the hanger as you would a regular joist hanger. Cut the end of the joist at 45 degrees and place it in the hanger. Close the other side of the hanger and drive nails through every nail hole in the joist hanger.

3

CUT EACH JOIST

Extend the marks from the chalk line down the faces of the interior joists with a speed square, and cut all the joists (except the header and rim joist) on the marks with a circular saw set for a 45-degree bevel. Mark the header and rim joists for an angle of 22½ degrees and cut these joists with the saw beveled at this angle.

4

MARK THE DIAGONAL HEADER

Set a board that is slightly longer than the span of the opening across the header and rim joists, lined up with the interior joists. Mark each end of the diagonal header where it intersects the header and rim joist. Cut the board to length with the circular saw bevel gauge set at 22½ degrees.

5

INSTALL THE DIAGONAL HEADER

Drive 3-inch deck screws through the diagonal header into the cut ends of the header and rim joist, making sure the screws penetrate the wood squarely. Install 45-degree hangers on all joists.

REAL WORLD

NOT ALL JOISTS ARE EQUAL

It seemed a lot more efficient to one builder to measure the width of a 2×10 and set all the joist hangers at one time. Some joists, however, ended up either higher or lower than the header. It turned out the joists weren't all the same width—there was a difference of more than ¼ inch in width from the widest to the narrowest. Redoing the job was not the most efficient use of time.

Trimming joists to length in place

As an alternative to building the perimeter frame and installing the interior joists, you can install the interior joists on the ledger and let their lengths run wild. This method will require you to trim all the joists to the same length at the same time, then fasten the header to the trimmed ends.

1

MARK THE JOIST LENGTH
Position the joists on the beam at their proper locations and brace them in place with a 1×4 fastened across the top edges. Snap a chalk line at the length of the joists.

2

DRAW CUTTING LINES
Extend the chalk line down the face of each joist with a layout square. Then mark another line on the face of the joists equivalent to the distance from the circular saw blade to the edge of the saw plate.

3

CUT ENDS WITH A GUIDE
Fasten a 1×4 cutting guide at each of the second lines you marked and trim each joist with a circular saw. Keep the edge of the saw plate firmly against the cutting guides throughout each cut.

4

ATTACH HEADER
Have a helper hold the header in place and fasten each end to the rim joists. Face-nail the header to each joist and strengthen the structure by installing joist hangers. Install blocking if needed (see opposite page) and attach joists to the beam with rafter ties.

5

FRAMING

Blocking the joists

Install blocking between joists to prevent twisting, especially on spans longer than 8 feet. Measure each piece of blocking separately to allow for any difference in the thickness of the joists. This will keep the blocking from bowing the joists.

Alternate blocking to make nailing easy.

1

MARK POSITION FOR BLOCKING
Snap a chalk line across joists at the center of the joists. This line locates the position for blocking pieces.

2

ATTACH BLOCKING
Fasten the blocking between the joists with 3-inch galvanized spiral-shank nails or 3-inch screws. Attach blocking between adjacent joists on opposite sides of the chalk line to allow you to face-nail the fasteners.

3

ATTACH JOISTS TO THE BEAM
Attach the joists to the beam with rafter/hurricane ties. Install ties on the less-visible side of the beam, if possible, driving the kind of nail specified by the manufacturer through every nail hole in the connector.

5

FRAMING

5

FRAMING

CLOSER LOOK

Nailing plate

Rafter/hurricane tie

Seismic/hurricane ties

TWO WAYS TO SPLICE JOISTS

Many deck designs require joists longer than are available in dimension lumber. Make a long joist by splicing two shorter pieces of 2× lumber together. The splice must be centered over a beam. One splicing method is to butt the ends of two boards over a beam (above, left). Make certain there is a tight fit between the boards. A nailing plate (see page 40) reinforces the joint, and rafter/hurricane ties attach the boards to the beam.

The other method overlaps the board ends over a beam (above, right). Boards should overlap 12 inches and are fastened together with 3-inch deck screws. A seismic/hurricane tie attaches each board to the beam. The butt joint method uses less wood and keeps the decking screws in a straight line. An overlap splice is quicker to make but creates an offset line of screws in the decking that you may find less attractive.

Installing joists around obstructions

PROJECT DETAILS

SKILLS: Measuring and cutting lumber, driving fasteners
PROJECT: Installing joists around a mature tree

TIME TO COMPLETE

EXPERIENCED: 20 min.
HANDY: 40 min.
NOVICE: 1 hr.

STUFF YOU'LL NEED

TOOLS: Tape measure, layout square, circular saw, hammer
MATERIALS: Lumber, fasteners, joist hangers

Framing around obstructions such as trees, rocks, or spas usually requires that at least one joist position be interrupted. The obstruction requires double joists around the obstacle in order to support the ends of the interrupted joists. Check with local code if your installation requires interrupting more than two joists; additional posts and beams may be necessary. Frame openings around trees to allow room for future growth. The diameter of the mature poplar trunk shown in this project will not increase significantly.

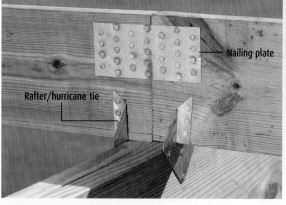

1 **DOUBLE-UP JOISTS**
Install double joists in double joist hangers on both sides of the obstruction. Attach the other joists following the usual method.

2 **INSTALL DOUBLE HEADERS**

Install double headers in double joist hangers on both sides of the obstruction between the double joists.

3 **INSTALL SHORT JOISTS**

Install the interrupted joists between the header or ledger and the double header. This keeps joist spacing consistent for the decking fasteners.

4 **ATTACH DECKING**

Cut the decking and attach it to the joists as shown in chapter 6. This is a mature tree and the diameter of the trunk will not increase significantly. You should allow more space around immature trees.

Installing a round or hexagonal opening

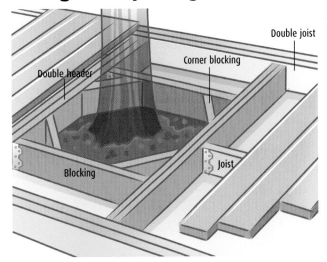

Double joist

Corner blocking

Double header

Joist

Blocking

MAKE A DECORATIVE OPENING

Set up your framing to allow for the installation of blocking and corner blocks. The corner blocks will support either a circular or hexagonal opening in the decking. For a circular opening, let the decking overhang the blocking. Then using a cardboard template equal to the arc of the opening, mark the circle on the decking and cut it with a jigsaw. Sand the edges smooth.

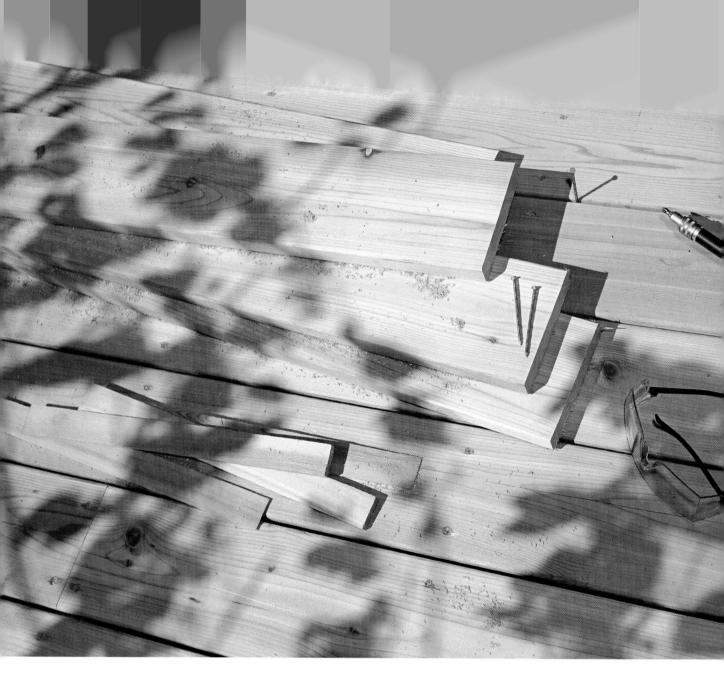

Decking

ecking is one of the most visible parts of the deck, so its installation deserves special care and attention. Choose good-looking boards and install them neatly for the best appearance. Use a sharp blade in a mitersaw or circular saw when cutting them so you get crisp edges without splinters.

Whether and how much you space the boards depends on what kind of material you're using. Kiln-dried lumber and naturally resistant species won't shrink much so you should space them at about ⅛ inch. Synthetic decking won't shrink either, but boards are usually spaced wider than

lumber. Check the manufacturer's instructions before you start installing synthetic decking. Pressure-treated lumber will shrink, so butt the edges together when you lay it.

You can start the first board on the header end or next to the house, but unless you are certain that the boards will cover the deck area without requiring you to rip the last one narrower, you should start at the front and work toward the house. That way the narrow board will be less visible.

Chapter 6 highlights

INSTALLING DECKING
Decking is the floor of your outdoor room and, as such, is one of the more visible elements of your deck.

108

INSTALLING DIAGONAL DECKING
Installing decking on the diagonal, like other alternate decking patterns, requires some changes in the basic joist system.

115

INSTALLING SYNTHETIC DECKING
Synthetic decking is made to look and install like wood, but a few products require special fastening techniques.

116

ALTERNATE FASTENING SYSTEMS
For years, deck fasteners were so visible they became an unavoidable aspect of the deck design. These days, however, there are a number of fasteners that keep the decking in place without being seen.

121

Stagger butt joints in the decking so they don't fall in a straight line. The joints will become part of the rhythm of the decking pattern, so it's even better to lay out the decking in a dry run and position the joints for the best effect. Or you can run extra framing under the center of the deck, install a feature board the width of the deck perpendicular to the decking, and butt the ends of the decking against it.

Installing decking

ecking is usually 2×4, 2×6, or ⁵⁄₄×6 boards installed on wide faces. There are several common installation patterns (see page 19). Extra blocking must be installed for some patterns so both ends of each board are supported. The more complicated the decking pattern, the more important it is to do a dry run before you cut boards to lay out the angles and joints. Arrange boards with the fewest possible end-to-end seams, and stagger the seams for the best appearance. For a small deck, buy lumber long enough to span the entire width of the deck.

Find boards that are as straight as possible. Installation can straighten a small amount of twisting or bowing. Return boards that are more than a little crooked. Buy about 10 percent more decking than you estimate is necessary to allow for returns and for cutting waste during installation. For diagonal patterns buy about 15 percent more.

Growth rings visible in the end grain of a decking board indicate which side of the board was closest to the bark side of the tree from which it came. Professional carpenters disagree whether the bark side should face up or down during installation. The best solution is to properly fasten each board so its best-looking side is visible. Deck screws make the strongest connection but have larger, more visible heads than nails (see page 38). Look for color screws that match decking. The cedar decking for the upper level on this project was installed perpendicular to the joists and fastened with deck screws.

1 **MEASURE THE DECK**
Measure between the outside of the header joist and the house at the top of the ledger. Do this at the center and ends of the deck to determine whether the distances are equal. Mark each rim joist at a distance from the outside of the header joist equal to the width of one decking board. (If your deck will have fascia boards, mark this distance from the outside face of the fascia attached to the header joist.) Make these marks at equal distances from the house. Note: Decking installation also can begin at the house with the final board attached at the header joist.

2

MARK THE FIRST BOARD'S POSITION

Snap a chalk line on the marks across the rim joists. Check to make sure this line is parallel to the house.

3

INSTALL THE FIRST BOARD

Align the inside edge of the first length of decking with the chalk line, letting the ends of the decking extend wild (at uneven lengths) beyond the rim joist. Drive two fasteners through the board into the center of each joist. Position each fastener ¾ to 1 inch from the edge of the board.

CLOSER LOOK

SPACING WOOD DECKING

Gaps between decking boards let water drain off and allow air to circulate around the decking. When using any lumber besides PT wood, space the boards at a consistent ⅛ inch. Use either 8d or 10d nails as spacers and tap one into each joist after fastening a length of decking. Butt the next board tightly against the nails before attaching it. Drive in the fasteners then remove the spacing nails.

You can also make a spacing jig from a 1×4 about 4 feet long (above, left). Snap a chalk line down the center of the strip and drive a nail every 16 inches at the chalk line so about 1 inch of the nail protrudes on the other side. Set the jig down (with the nail points between joists). Another easy-to-use spacer is a long metal straightedge (above, right) that is about ⅛ inch thick. Set the edge of the straightedge between boards.

4

INSTALL ROW 2

Install the next row of boards. Position spacers (page 109) for a ⅛-inch gap. Butt each board against the spacers before fastening. If you have to use more than one board per row, center the ends over the joists.

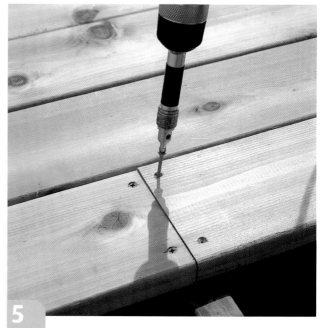

5

PREDRILL AT ENDS

Drive fasteners through predrilled holes at the ends of boards. Predrilling prevents splitting of the wood by either screws or nails. Boards should meet at the center of the joist. Angle each fastener toward the center of the joist.

CLOSER LOOK

GETTING THE FASTENERS FLUSH

Drive each deck screw so the head surface is flush with the surface of the board. A screw driven too deeply creates an unattractive depression that collects moisture and debris. Use screws long enough to penetrate into the joists as deep as the thickness of the decking. For example, use 3 or 3½-inch screws to attach 2× decking. Buy an inexpensive depth-setting attachment for your drill so screwheads can be set consistently flush with the decking surface.

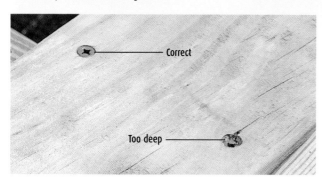

Correct

Too deep

6

MEASURE AGAIN

Measure from the back edge of the third row of decking to the house at several spots. Boards may vary in width so the distances may not be equal (they frequently aren't).

7

PRY TO KEEP SPACES EVEN

Use a pry bar to pull a board toward the spacers, if necessary. Stick the points of the long end of the pry bar into the joist with the bar against the edge of the board. Pull on the pry bar to force the board against the spacers.

WORK SMARTER

FORCING BOARDS INTO PLACE

Drive fasteners partway into a board before you force it into position. Align the fasteners over the joist and drive them until the points are almost through the board. Force the board against the spacer and finish driving the fasteners. This is much easier than trying to start a fastener into a board while pulling on a pry bar. Instead of a pry bar, you can use a pipe clamp or bar clamp to pull a board into position. Stick the bent end of the pry bar between decking boards to anchor the clamp. To prevent damage when prying a board, insert a wide putty knife behind the pry bar.

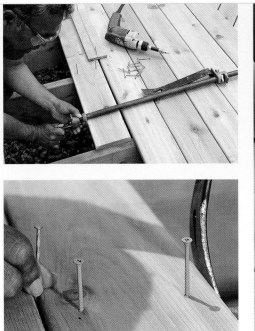

6

8

PUT CROWN TOWARD PREVIOUS BOARD
Install a slightly bowed board with the crown edge against the previously installed board. First position one end of the new board against the spacers.

9

FASTEN END OF BOARD
Drive two fasteners at the end of the board. Make certain the board is tightly against the spacers before driving the fasteners.

10

FASTEN THE SPACED END
Install fasteners in the last joist where the board is firmly against the spacer.

WORK SMARTER

NEAT NAILING TIPS
Hammer spiral shank nails at an angle to give them more holding power. Angled fasteners will leave one side of the head deeper than the other, however, and you may not like the appearance. Blunt the point of a nail before driving it. Rest the nailhead on a hard surface and strike the point with a hammer. A blunt nail won't split the wood as easily as a sharp point will.

DECKING

11

FORCE END INTO POSITION

Insert spacers along the remaining length of the board, force the far end into position, and attach it to the joist. Then drive fasteners at the remaining joist positions.

 DESIGN TIP

USE LESS LUMBER

To save decking when installing box steps on a multilevel deck, you don't need to install decking under the steps.

12

LAY OUT NOTCH AROUND POST

Mark notches around obstacles such as railing posts or legs for built-in benches. Position a board against the obstacle, aligning the board ends properly. Use a layout square to complete the outline.

13

JIGSAW THE NOTCH

Cut the notch with a jigsaw. Make the cuts on the outside of the marked lines to provide room for a good fit around the obstacle and still leave a little space for drainage and expansion. Cut from both directions into the notch corners to make square corners.

6

DECKING

14 PUT CLEAT ON POST

Install a 2×4 nailing cleat to support the edge of a notched board. Make the cleat from pressure-treated wood for durability.

15 TEST-FIT AND ATTACH

Test-fit the notched board, enlarging the notch, if necessary, by trimming small amounts of material with a jigsaw or chisel. Then attach the board with fasteners driven into joists and nailing cleats.

16 PUT IN THE LAST BOARD

Measure the space at both ends of the last row and rip the last board to fit, if necessary. Rip the board ¼ inch narrower than the measurement to leave a ⅛-inch gap between the board and the siding to prevent trapping moisture. Crosscut the board so it will be flush with the rim joists on both ends. The last row can't be cut in place because the wall prevents a saw from completing the cut.

17 TRIMMING THE ENDS, OPTION A:

Use the end of the last decking board (that was cut to length before installing) and the corner of the deck at the header as reference points and snap a chalk line between them. Trim the decking on the chalk line with a circular saw. Set the saw to the proper depth so it just goes through the boards.

OPTION B:

Snap the chalkline as in option A and tack a long, straight 1×4 to the decking as a guide for a circular saw. Position the guide so the saw blade will trim boards on the chalk line. Use this technique if you're not sure you can make a long, straight freehand cut.

Installing diagonal decking

Equal distance

LAY OUT A DIAGONAL LINE

Snap a diagonal chalk line near the center of the deck area (above, left). Measure and mark equal distances from the deck corner to establish a diagonal line at 45 degrees. Install the first board aligned with the line. Follow the basic decking installation methods shown on the previous pages. Snap a new chalk line after every three rows of decking (above, right). Measure from the edge of the board aligned with the first diagonal chalk line to keep the decking at a consistent angle. Install boards on one half of the deck, then return to the first diagonal line and install the remaining decking. Let the boards hang over the framing, and trim to the proper length after installation.

CLOSER LOOK

ACCESS HATCH BLENDS INTO DECK SURFACE

Build an access hatch for a hose bib or other item beneath the decking surface. Attach 12-inch-long cleats cut from pressure-treated 2×4s to the joists on both sides of the item (below). The top of the cleats should be 3½ inches below the tops of the joists. Build a box frame from pressure-treated 2×4s. The frame length is equal to the distance between the joists minus ¼ inch. The frame width is equal to the width of the two decking boards in the last two rows next to the house. Remember to include the ⅛-inch gap between them. Use screws to fasten the frame pieces together. Cover the frame with pieces of decking cut to size (left). Drill two 1-inch-diameter finger holes so you can grip the hatch to open it.

Installing synthetic decking

6

DECKING

ike its wood counterparts, synthetic decking needs a strong, stable frame under it, so preparation for synthetic decking is no different than for a deck with wood decking. Build your frame from pressure-treated lumber as you would any other deck.

Storage of synthetic decking is similar to any other material, but you must support it every 2 feet. You should not stack most synthetic materials higher than six units or 12 feet high.

As with any construction project, you should wear the proper protective clothing and safety equipment. Composite decking is heavier and more flexible than wood. Do not try to lift the same number of synthetic boards as you would traditional lumber.

As with all materials, synthetic decking must be spaced to allow for expansion and proper circulation. Some synthetic products require a substantially wider gap (¼ to ⅜ inch) between boards.

Installing composite decking

1

MARK EDGE OF FIRST BOARD

Measure from the house to the position of the inside edge of the starter board, and mark each end of the header at this distance. Where this line falls will depend on whether and how much you want it to overhang the header. Snap a chalk line across the marks on the rim joists. Check to make sure this line is parallel to the house. Begin decking installation with boards parallel to the house.

Decking overhangs framing with wild lengths.

1" from edge of decking

2

ATTACH THE FIRST BOARD

Lay out the decking boards loosely on the deck so they're within reach. Plan staggered joints ahead, prearranging the boards and installing cleats on both sides of the joists where necessary. Align the inside edge of the starter board with the chalk line and face-nail or screw two fasteners centered on the joists. Predrill holes for the fastener if recommended by the manufacturer.

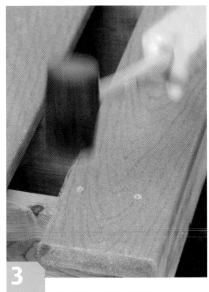

3 TAP DOWN MUSHROOMS

Smooth out mushrooming around fasteners (especially screws) by tapping the decking with a rubber mallet. Some composite materials may require that you use a regular hammer. Check the manufacturer's directions for specific instructions.

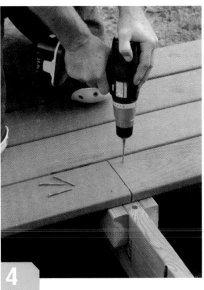

4 SUPPORT JOINTS WITH CLEATS

Where butt joints are necessary, strengthen each joint by fastening 2×4 cleats on both sides of the joist. Predrill the decking to minimize splitting.

5 MAINTAIN SPACING

Continue fastening the decking using the techniques shown on pages 108–114, maintaining the spacing between boards recommended by the manufacturer. When you get within three boards of the last one, dry-lay the boards, maintaining spacing. If the last board fits without trimming, install the remaining decking. If not, lay two boards and trim the last one. Or rip the three boards to equal widths. Trim the last board to length for the overhang; you can't trim it in place.

6 INSTALL FASCIA

Attach fascia boards over the framing with two screws every 18 inches.

CLOSER LOOK

USING COMPOSITE SCREWS

Composite decking screws are made for use with composite materials. They are self-tapping screws with a barrel head. Most manufacturers claim that the screw needs no predrilling and won't mushroom the decking surface like other fasteners. If your particular material behaves otherwise, predrill the holes and level the mushrooming as shown in Step 3, above.

Installing composite decking with deck clips

1 ATTACH FIRST BOARD

Lay the first board by face-nailing or screwing it as shown on page 116. Position the clip on the joists with the points touching the rear edge of the board. Using a hammer and the tapping block provided by the manufacturer, force the clip into the board.

2 INSTALL CLIPS

Drive the fastener provided by the manufacturer into the joist with a cordless drill. Continue installing the clips on the joists along the remaining length of the board.

3 DRIVE BOARD ONTO CLIPS

Line up the next board next to the one already installed, and drive the board into the clips with a heavy sledge, protecting the edge of the decking with a 2×4. Continue setting the rest of the decking.

Installing synthetic decking with T-clips

1 SET HEADER HIGHER

Fasten the header so its top front edge is ⅞ inch higher than the top of the other joists. This will give the bullnose cap a surface on which to lock.

2 INSTALL BULLNOSE CAP

Set the bullnose cap in place on the header, notching the bullnose for posts as necessary. Predrill the foot of the bullnose at a joist roughly in the center of its length, and drive a screw through the foot and into the joist.

3 INSTALL T-CLIP

Hold the T-clip snugly against the rear edge of the bullnose and drive the fastener through the hole and into the joists. Install T-clips on the remaining joists along the length of the bullnose cap.

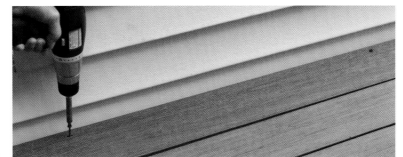

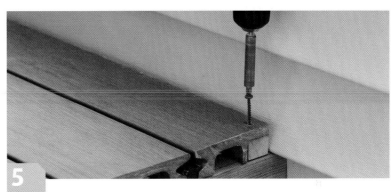

4 INSTALL SECOND BOARD

Slide the second board firmly against the T-clips on the first board, and drive a screw into the center of the foot into a predrilled hole—the same as you did in the bullnose. Install T-clips on the joists along the second board. Continue installing the remaining boards until you reach the last board.

5 ADD FILLER FOR LAST BOARD

Fasten the last board to the ledger with screws every 36 inches. Slot all the holes (use a rotary hand tool) except the center one to allow for adequate expansion. If you have to rip the last board to fit next to the house (leave the gap specified by the manufacturer), support the cut flange along its length with a piece of ripped stock.

CLOSER LOOK

To install a T-clip securely, push it firmly against the foot of the previous board and predrill the fastener hole. Keeping the T-clip in place, drive the fastener through the clip into the joist. Install the remaining clips along the length of the board and snug the next board firmly against the clips that are in place. Continue to install the rest of the clips in the same manner.

6 FINISH WITH FASCIA

Cover the exposed ends of the decking and the space between the bullnose lip and the front header joists with the fascia recommended by the manufacturer.

Curved composite decking

Some kinds of composite decking can be bent into curves, which adds a design capability not readily available with any other material. Some composites can be curved without additional heat in temperatures above 80°F. Others require warming with a heat source and blower fan. Be sure to check with the manufacturer or retailer before using an additional heat source to bend the decking. Too much heat might melt the material. Uneven heat could turn your gentle curves into sharp corners.

1

LAY OUT THE CURVE

Mark the curvature on the joists. Tack 2× blocks to the top of the joists along the circumference of the innermost curve. Fasten the end of the first board with its rear edge against the 2× block, and bend it slowly toward the next 2× block. Fasten the board at this joist and continue the process until the first board is in place, curved against the blocks.

2

PLACE THE SECOND BOARD

Fasten the end of the second board and insert a spacing tool (provided by the manufacturer) between the first and second board just beyond the next joist. Have a helper put pressure on the board till the curve is just beyond the spacing tool. Then fasten the board to the next joist.

3

MAINTAIN SPACING

Keep the spacing tool in place and insert a second spacing tool between the boards just beyond the next joist.

4

CONTINUE UNTIL CURVE IS COMPLETE

Fasten the next board and continue this process until you have completed the entire curved section.

Alternate fastening systems

PROJECT DETAILS

SKILLS: Measuring and cutting lumber, driving fasteners
PROJECT: Using deck clips to install decking on a 16×12-foot deck, assuming you have a helper

TIME TO COMPLETE

EXPERIENCED: 5 hrs.
HANDY: 6 hrs.
NOVICE: 7 hrs.

STUFF YOU'LL NEED

TOOLS: Tape measure, layout square, power mitersaw, drill, pry bar, hammer
MATERIALS: Lumber, fasteners, clip or track system hardware

Several systems fasten decking to joists invisibly. The two basic types are clip systems and track systems. Clip systems (pages 121–123) typically fasten decking with small metal clips installed between board edges. Track systems (page 123) fasten the undersides of boards to metal track sections installed on the joists.

Fastening decking with either of these systems takes significantly more time than driving fasteners through the face of the decking. The additional hardware also increases the cost of the deck, but using one of these systems results in a deck surface with no visible fasteners.

Check the instructions for an alternate system before purchasing decking. Some decking systems require 2× lumber. Make certain decking lumber is dry when using a clip system. Wet lumber will shrink and pull away from the clips. Many of these systems are usable with both wood and synthetic decking, but be sure to check the manufacturer before using one with a synthetic product.

Deck clips

1

SCREW OR NAIL FIRST ROW
Fasten the first row of decking to the header by toenailing with 10d galvanized nails or 3-inch decking screws at every joist. Drill pilot holes for the fasteners to prevent splitting the board edge.

2

ATTACH CLIPS TO BOARD
Attach clips to one edge of the next board, positioned within 2 inches of every joist. Attach clips with fasteners recommended by the clip manufacturer.

Deck clips *(continued)*

3 SLIDE CLIPS UNDER BOARD

Hold each board at a slight angle, and slide the clips under the edge of the first row of decking. Push boards as far forward as possible before placing them flat on the joists.

4 SEAT THE BOARD

Use a hammer and a scrap wood block to seat each board firmly against the first row. The clips automatically create the proper gap between boards.

5 TOENAIL BACK EDGE

Toenail through the back edge of the second row of boards. Drill pilot holes before driving fasteners. Make certain each board clip is firmly against the adjacent board before fastening. Use the methods shown on page 111 to force a bowed board into position. Continue installing rows of decking.

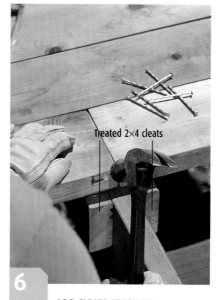

Treated 2×4 cleats

6 ADD CLEATS AT JOINTS

Add cleats to fasten a board end at butt joints. Position the clip for the board in the next row within 2 inches of one of the cleats so the cleats won't obstruct the clip.

7 FACE-NAIL FINAL ROW

Drive nails through the face of the boards in the last row of decking. If you have to force the last row into position, protect the siding with a piece of scrap wood between the pry bar and siding. Use a nail set to drive nailheads beneath the surface of the boards. Fill the holes with exterior putty or colored caulk.

Biscuit clips

1 CUT CLIP RECESSES

Biscuit clips attach to the joists and grip slots cut in the edges of the decking. Lay out the decking on the joists or any flat surface with their edges lined up. Snap chalk lines across the boards at intervals equal to your joist spacing. Using a biscuit joiner, cut slots for the clips into the decking at each chalk line. Cut the slots in both edges of every board, except the first and last ones.

2 INSTALL FIRST BOARD

Fasten the first board as prescribed by the manufacturer of the biscuits (generally by face-nailing). Then center the clip on the joist and push it into the slot in the decking. Holding the clip in place, drive in the fastener as specified by the clip manufacturer. Complete the installation of clips across the length of the first board. Push the next board into place and repeat.

Track system

ATTACH TRACK TO JOISTS

Short pieces of metal track are attached to the joists with fasteners supplied by the manufacturer (above, left). Position them according to manufacturer's instructions. A common method is to attach sections on alternate sides of each joist. Cut track to length with aviation snips when necessary. Position the decking on top of the joists, maintaining the proper spacing. Drive fasteners through holes in the metal track and into the decking (above, right). Work from underneath the deck, if possible, to avoid awkward positioning.

Building stairs and ramps

Stairs connect a deck to the surrounding landscape and join levels in multilevel decks. A stair may be a single step up to a low-level deck or the next level in a multilevel design or a long flight to an elevated deck. The principles and methods for making stringers shown on these pages are basic to all stairs. Plan stair locations carefully to make the best use of space and traffic patterns. Check local codes for width, rise, and run requirements before finalizing your plans. For safety, consider installing solid risers when the rise between steps is more than 4 inches.

The ascent should be gradual for outdoor stairs—what you need are short risers and deep treads. A simple rule makes stair design easy: twice

Chapter 7 highlights

MAKING STRINGERS
Stringers are the diagonal part of a stairs that holds the treads. You must make them carefully to have a stable, comfortable transition from place to place and level to level.

128

BUILDING STAIRS WITH A LANDING
Climbing a long stairs can be tiring. Why not break up the journey into smaller parts by adding a landing? This section shows you how.

134

WRAPPING STAIRS AROUND A CORNER
Some deck designs require steps that extend from the deck in two directions. All it takes to pull this off is a little special framing.

138

BUILDING AN ACCESS RAMP
Access ramps are really angled decks and their construction involves many of the same methods as a deck—everything is just on an incline.

139

the riser height (the height of each step to the top of the tread) plus its run (the front-to-back depth of the tread) should equal between 24 and 27 inches.

Start by measuring the total rise and run for your stairs. You can plan a specific location for the stairway landing pad and cut stringers to meet it.

Or you can decide how many steps and what rise and run you want, then position the pad according to your calculations. Even better is to start with a prospective pad location and estimate whether the resulting rise and run will be comfortable and aesthetically pleasing. Then get out the pencil and paper and do the math (see page 127).

CALCULATING STAIR MEASUREMENTS

Transferring stairs from a building plan to the building site requires that you know the exact distances involved. Determine the height required for the stairs based on the structure you build. Measure from the top of the decking to ground level at the stair location (photo 1). Use the information on the opposite page to calculate the distance from the deck to the end of the stair. Place a long straight board in the direction the stair will run and measure out this distance. Use a level to check ground slope relative to the bottom of the deck (photo 2). Then measure from the bottom of the board if the ground slopes away from the deck (photo 3). Add this measurement to the deck height measurement. Calculate the stair tread and riser measurements necessary to make the stair stringers (opposite page). Adjust the overall stair run and ending point of the stairs, if necessary.

Computing the rise and run of steps

For easier climbs, exterior stairs should have shorter rises and deeper treads than interior stairs. The standard formula is: Twice the unit rise plus the unit run should equal between 24 and 27 inches. For example, stairs with a unit rise of 7 inches and a unit run of 11 inches meet this criteria ($2 \times 7 = 14$; $14 + 11 = 25$).

To calculate rise and run, measure the total rise of the stairs (see box, opposite and illustration below) and divide it by the height you want for each step. Round to the nearest whole number; this is the number of rises. Then divide the total rise by the number of rises to find the exact rise for each step.

Here's how it works with real numbers. Assume the total rise is 58 inches and you want each step to be about 7 inches high. Dividing 58 by 7 = 8.28. Round that to 8 steps. Dividing 58 by 8 steps gives you a unit rise of 7.25 inches. To find the exact length of the stairway, multiply the run you want (11 inches) by the number of rises minus one (remember, the last rise is up to the deck surface). In this case $7 \times 11 = 77$. So the stairway will end 77 inches away from the deck.

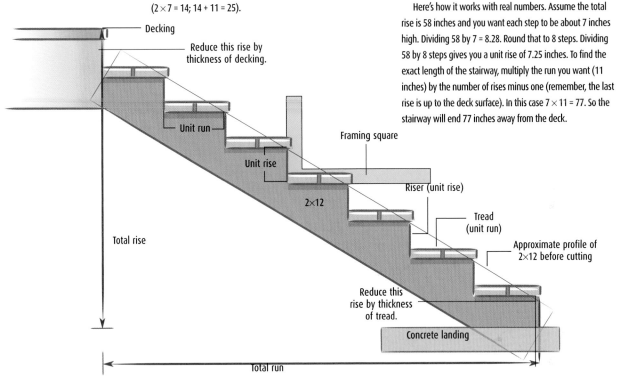

- Decking
- Reduce this rise by thickness of decking.
- Unit run
- Unit rise
- 2×12
- Total rise
- Reduce this rise by thickness of tread.
- Framing square
- Riser (unit rise)
- Tread (unit run)
- Approximate profile of 2×12 before cutting
- Concrete landing
- Total run

OPEN STRINGERS

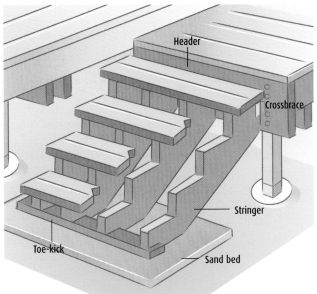

- Header
- Crossbrace
- Stringer
- Toe-kick
- Sand bed

CLOSED STRINGERS

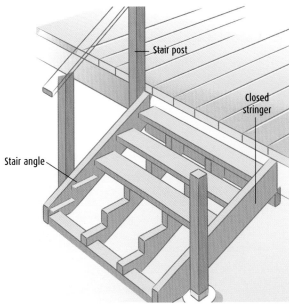

- Stair post
- Closed stringer
- Stair angle

Making stringers

PROJECT DETAILS

SKILLS: Measuring and cutting lumber, laying out a pattern, driving fasteners
PROJECT: Making three stringers, for a deck 8 feet off the ground

TIME TO COMPLETE

EXPERIENCED: 2 hrs.
HANDY: 3 hrs.
NOVICE: 4 hrs.

STUFF YOU'LL NEED

TOOLS: Tape measure, framing square, stair gauges, circular saw, jigsaw, drill, ratchet and socket, random orbital sander
MATERIALS: Lumber, fasteners, preservative

7

BUILDING STAIRS AND RAMPS

There are two types of stringers: *Open stringers*, also called cut stringers, have notches for steps cut into them. The treads are attached to the notches. *Closed stringers* use cleats (or metal stair angles) attached to their inner faces to support the treads. The style you choose is largely a matter of personal choice, style, and how much time you want to devote to making the stringers. Open stringers take a little more time than closed ones.

Plan to build deck stairs at least 3 feet wide for ease of traffic flow and safe use. Most codes require a 3-foot minimum stair width anyway. On wide stairs, additional stringers are installed between outer stringers for support. These interior stringers must be open stringers even if you use closed stringers for the outer ones.

Install extra open stringers about every 16 inches on wider stairs when using ⁵⁄₄-inch-thick lumber for treads, and every 24 inches for 2× lumber.

Use the best 2×12 boards you can find for stringers. Open stringers should be cut from pressure-treated lumber. Remember to apply preservative to the cut edges. Many codes allow wood other than pressure-treated for closed stringers.

Open stringers

Run

Stair gauge

Rise

1

SET STAIR MEASUREMENTS ON SQUARE
Lay the framing square on the stringer board so the unit run measurement on the outside of the wide body of the square intersects the edge of the board. Clamp a stair gauge on the inside edge of the leg so it won't interfere with marking. Set the length of the unit rise on the outer edge of the narrow leg so it intersects the edge of the board. Clamp on a stair gauge to hold the measurement.

2
LAY OUT THE TOP STEP
Mark the rise and the run for the first step at the top end of the stringer. Place the framing square on the board for the stringer with the gauges resting against what will be the top edge. Intersect the corner of the board with the rise line. The rise measurement at the top end of the stringer sets the stringer at the correct distance from the decking surface.

📖 WORK SMARTER

Stair gauges

IT'S EASY TO BE CONSISTENT
Stair gauges, also known as stair buttons, are inexpensive pairs of small metal guides used to make stair stringers. They clamp onto a framing square and make it simple to mark consistent rise and run measurements. Mark rise with the short leg of the square and mark run with the long leg.

3
MARK THE TOP CUTTING LINE
Extend the rise line to the bottom edge of the stringer. Mark an 'X' in waste areas to prevent confusion when you start cutting.

4
LAY OUT THE NEXT STEP
Mark the rise and run for the next step. Slide the framing square down the stringer edge until the rise line touches the point where the tread line from the previous step intersects the board edge. Make certain the stair gauges rest against the board. Repeat this process to mark all steps.

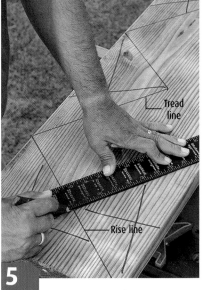

Tread line

Rise line

5
MARK THE BOTTOM STEP
Place the framing square on the opposite edge of the board to mark the bottom end of the stringer. The stair gauges must rest against the board edge to maintain proper alignment. First extend the final rise line across the end of the board. Then mark a line the distance of the rise from the tread line on the last step.

Open stringers *(continued)*

6 MARK THE CUTTING LINE

Mark another line below the last line, at a distance equal to the thickness of the tread. This is the bottom of the stringer. Subtracting the tread thickness from the first riser will leave the first step up from the ground at a comfortable height.

7 CUT THE STRINGER

Start cutting the stringer at the top end on the extended rise line. Then make the top tread cut. Use a sharp blade in a circular saw to make crisp cuts with clean edges.

8 STOP AT THE LINE

When making the cuts, stop the saw blade just before it reaches the corner.

9 FINISH CUT WITH A JIGSAW

Complete the cuts in the corner with a jigsaw, cutting along the outside of the kerf to remove all the waste.

10 TRACE THE NEXT STRINGER

Use the completed stringer as a template to mark boards for the remaining stringers. First hold the completed stringer in place to check for accuracy. Then clamp the template stringer to each board to keep the marking accurate.

7

BUILDING STAIRS AND RAMPS

ADDING A TOE-KICK

A toe-kick is an option for attaching the bottom ends of stringers to a concrete pad. Check local codes to determine how thick the pad must be. Make the toe-kick from 2×4 pressure-treated lumber. Fasten it to the pad with the same type of threaded rods, nuts, and washers used to attach post anchors to footings (see page 80). Epoxy bonds the rods into holes drilled in the pad. Cure fresh concrete for at least 48 hours before installing the rods.

REAL WORLD

WHEN A MISTAKE HAPPENS, THINK ABOUT IT
Mistakes can happen. Here's how careful analysis of the situation saved one builder from a costly redo: "When I began making stringers, I found the landing location was off on one side by over an inch," the builder reported. "Fortunately I realized that I could attach another layer of rim joist on that side. I had to replace some decking; but once I did, it was almost impossible to tell that I had even made a mistake!"

BUYER'S GUIDE

SIMPLIFY WITH PRECUT STRINGERS
Precut open stringers in various sizes, available at many home building centers, can simplify stair installation if you find a size that fits your deck. Check each stringer for defects before purchasing.

WORK SMARTER

MAKING THE BOTTOM CUT

OPTION A: Finish all of the step cuts and make the cut for the bottom of the stringer. This completes the stringer if the bottom will be attached directly to the landing pad with brackets (see page 136).

OPTION B: Mark a notch in the bottom end of the stringer to accommodate a toe-kick (see above and page 127). Size the notch to fit over the horizontal 2× stock used for the toe-kick.

Closed stringers

1 TRACE AN OPEN STRINGER

If your closed stringers will be used in conjunction with open stringers, cut an open stringer first and use it as a template to mark the closed stringers. Position the template with the step corners set back from the edge of a closed stringer board by the thickness of the tread.

2 LAY OUT CLOSED STRINGERS

Mark the tread positions on the closed stringer. Although you can mark the rise lines also (as shown here), they're unnecessary. You need only the tread lines for mounting the stair angles. Cut the extended riser line at the top end of the stringer. Then cut the bottom of the stringer to conform to the method you'll use to attach stringers to the landing pad (see page 131).

3 ATTACH STAIR ANGLES

Install the stringers in their proper locations and fasten a stair angle at each tread location on the closed stringers. You could use 2×2 wood cleats instead.

4 PUT STAIR ANGLES ON OPEN STRINGERS

Attach a stair angle at each tread on the open stringers. Using stair angles on the open stringers provides an invisible connection. Install the stair angles on opposite sides of the stringer, every other tread.

7

BUILDING STAIRS AND RAMPS

5 ATTACH STAIRS FROM UNDERSIDE

Drive fasteners recommended by the manufacturer (usually short lag screws) through the stair angles into the undersides of the treads.

6 USE SOCKET WRENCH WHERE DRILL WON'T REACH

Use a ratchet and an appropriate-size socket to drive fasteners in spaces too small to use the drill.

○ CLOSER LOOK

FINAL TREAD TREATMENTS

Treads may be installed with the ends overlapping the outer edges of open stringers by 1 inch (above, left), which is an attractive alternative to installing the ends flush with the outer edges. Round over the edges of the treads with a power sander, such as a random orbital sander (above, right).

Building stairs with a landing

PROJECT DETAILS

SKILLS: Measuring and layout, digging and pouring footings, cutting lumber, driving fasteners
PROJECT: Building stairs with one landing

TIME TO COMPLETE

EXPERIENCED: 1 day
HANDY: 1.5 days
NOVICE: 2 days

STUFF YOU'LL NEED

TOOLS: Tape measure, line level, water level, chalk line, shovel, power auger, posthole digger, maul, hammer, masonry finishing tools, speed square, circular saw, jigsaw, drill, ratchet and socket
MATERIALS: Lumber, fasteners, spikes, premix concrete, angle brackets, skewable joist hangers, stair cleats

U sing a landing to break up a long stair run makes the stairs easier and safer to traverse. You can also build a landing to change the direction of the stair run. In either case, all sections of a stairway must be constructed with the same rises and runs throughout.

Build the stairs at least 3 feet wide with either open or closed stringers on the ends—as your style determines. Stringers used as central supports must be open stringers. Install permanent bracing on posts for small stair landings to provide stability.

Make treads from the same material as your decking and with the same spacing. Because exterior stair treads are deeper from front to back, they offer you a chance to adjust the width of the treads. For example, two 2×6s with a ¼-inch gap between them will fit an 11-inch tread run with a slight overhang at the front of the step. You can use three 2×4s with the same spacing and there will be no overhang.

If you're constructing stairs in just a single section, use the instructions for the lower-stair run on the following pages.

1 **FINISH DECKING FIRST**
Install and trim the decking before starting the installation of the stairs. Lay out and pour any footings needed for the landing platform and install the landing pad. Compute the rise and run of both sections of the stairs (see page 127).

2

BUILD THE PLATFORM

Build the landing platform using the same techniques you would use for a deck (the platform is, in fact, a miniature deck). Install and plumb the posts, build the perimeter frame, hang joists in joist hangers, and attach the decking—with the same orientation and pattern as the deck, if possible.

3

MAKE LOWER-STAIR STRINGERS

Make stringers for the lower stairs using your earlier computations for the rise and run and employing the methods shown on pages 128-133.

4

ATTACH CLEATS FOR CROSSBRACE

Attach 2×4 cleats to the backside of the rim joist that faces the concrete pad. These cleats will support the crossbrace to which you will attach the stringers. The length of these cleats should equal the combined height of the rim joist, the unit rise, plus ½ inch (so the crossbrace will extend beneath the stringer).

5

INSTALL THE CROSSBRACE

Fasten the crossbrace (2× pressure-treated lumber) to the cleats with deck screws. Cut the nailer to length and width from 2× pressure-treated lumber. Install a crossbrace on the upper rim joists for the upper-stair run also.

7

BUILDING STAIRS AND RAMPS

6 INSTALL CENTER STRINGERS

Attach the center stringers with slopeable joist hangers (page 40). Level the tops of the stringers.

7 INSTALL OUTER STRINGERS

Connect each outer stringer to the crossbrace with an angle bracket, making sure the tread lines are level with each other and the center stringers.

8 MARK POSITION ON PAD

Mark the location of the bottom end of each stringer on the concrete pad, making sure the spacing between stringers is consistent throughout.

9 ATTACH STRINGERS TO PAD

Fasten an angle bracket to the pad with self-tapping masonry screws in predrilled holes. Anchor the stringers to the brackets with the nails recommended by the manufacturer.

10 INSTALL TREADS

Cut treads from the same material as the decking and fasten them to the stair angles with short lag screws (or the fasteners recommended by the manufacturer).

11 CUT UPPER-STAIR STRINGERS

Cut stringers for the upper-stair run and mark their locations on both sides of the landing. Snap a chalk line across the landing at the marks.

12
ATTACH TOE-KICK
Cut a toe-kick (a pressure-treated 2×4) so it will fit between the stringers and attach it to the landing with its front edge on the chalk line.

13
NOTCH STRINGERS FOR TOE-KICK
Cut a notch in the bottom end of the center stringer to accommodate the toe-kick.

14
ATTACH STRINGERS TO DECK
Attach each outer stringer to the upper deck with angle brackets. Install the center stringer in a slopeable joist hanger.

15
ATTACH STRINGERS TO TOE-KICK
Drive two deck screws through each outer stringer into the toe-kick. Toenail the center stringer to the toe-kick with deck screws.

Crossbrace

16
INSTALL STAIR ANGLES
Attach stair angles to the stringers as you did for the lower-stair run.

17
INSTALL TREADS
Drive fasteners through the cleats and into the undersides of the treads.

7

BUILDING STAIRS AND RAMPS

Wrapping stairs around a corner

PROJECT DETAILS

SKILLS: Measuring and cutting lumber, laying out a pattern, driving fasteners

PROJECT: Wrapping stairs with three steps around one corner

TIME TO COMPLETE

EXPERIENCED: 2 hrs.
HANDY: 3.5 hrs.
NOVICE: 5 hrs.

STUFF YOU'LL NEED

TOOLS: Tape measure, speed square, level, framing square, stair gauges, circular saw, jigsaw, drill
MATERIALS: Lumber, fasteners

Wraparound stairs can be incorporated into any deck structure, but they are an addition more easily accomplished on decks less than 4 feet tall. Open stringers (pages 128–131) are easier to accomplish for this stair style, which also requires a stringer that projects out from the corner. The length of the treads must be long enough to span from the end stringers to the middle of the diagonal stringer.

Wraparound stairs work best on a deck less than 4 feet tall.

Corner stringer will be placed here.

1

INSTALL SIDE STRINGERS

Install a stringer on each side of the deck corner. Make one face of each stringer flush with the corner. Space the remaining stringers on both sides of the deck according to the tread thickness. Anchor the bottom ends of the stringers with toe-kicks (page 127).

2

ADD DIAGONAL STRINGER

Cut and install the diagonal stringer. Miter cut the treads so they will meet at the center of the diagonal stringer. Attach them with screws in predrilled holes.

Building an access ramp

PROJECT DETAILS

SKILLS: Measuring and marking a pattern, cutting lumber, driving fasteners, installing concrete
PROJECT: Building an 8-foot-long access ramp

TIME TO COMPLETE

EXPERIENCED: 6 hrs.
HANDY: 8 hrs.
NOVICE: 10 hrs.
(Does not include drying time)

STUFF YOU'LL NEED

TOOLS: Tape measure, speed square, straightedge, maul, circular saw, jigsaw, drill, masonry tools
MATERIALS: Lumber, fasteners, premix concrete, joist hangers

A ramp provides more comfortable access for persons whose mobility is impaired.

All ramps will terminate at a landing (basically a small deck), and the location of the entire structure should be at the entrance to the house that offers the most convenient access to the interior. If the door opens toward the landing, allow at least 4 feet beyond the open door. Also direct roof runoff away from the ramp and landing with a gutter and downspout.

Build an access ramp with the same methods used to build a deck, including stair layout and construction techniques. The only differences are: The "deck platform" of the ramp is sloped and stringers supporting a ramp section that reaches ground level are tapered. Leave a ⅛-inch gap between decking boards so water will drain from the ramp.

Build a concrete landing pad at the beginning of the ramp. Slope the ramp no more than 1 inch of rise for every 12 inches of run (called 1-in-12 slope). A more gradual slope may be necessary due to terrain, distance from the house, or the abilities of the person using it.

Minimum ramp width is 36 inches but a 42- to 48-inch-wide ramp with railings is usually best for wheelchair access. Railings should have a graspable handrail (see page 153). A curb (a piece of wood installed at an outer ramp edge at least 2 inches higher than the ramp surface) may also be required. Check with your local code officials for specific regulations in your area.

Cut stringers for ramps that are less than 10 feet long from boards wide enough to eliminate the need for posts. Longer ramps require footings and posts to support stringers and landings. The ramp to the 8-inch-high deck in this project is 96 inches long (a 1-in-12 slope).

1 MARK END OF RAMP

Measure from the end of the deck to the concrete pad or sidewalk and mark the end point of the ramp. To calculate the end point of the ramp, measure the height of the deck from ground level. Then calculate the run length necessary for the deck height.

2 LAY OUT AND CUT ONE STRINGER

Lay out the slope on one board. Make the narrow tip of the stringer 1½ inches high. Lay out a ¾x4-inch notch in the bottom edge of the narrow end to fit over a cleat. Cut out the notch with a jigsaw and make the long cuts with a circular saw. Then use this stringer as a template for the others.

Cut the 5° bevel on this edge first

1½ in.

3 MAKE THE BOTTOM CLEAT

Cut a 1½-inch-wide strip from 1x6 pressure-treated lumber. First adjust the blade angle on the circular saw and cut a 5-degree bevel on one edge of the board. Then cut the strip so the widest face is 1½ inches. Make the strip as long as the ramp is wide.

DESIGN TIP

RAMP LANDINGS

Include a landing in an access ramp that rises more than 3 feet so you have a resting place within a long run. Make the landing at least 4 feet long. A landing where turning is required should be 5 feet long. Construct long ramps along the length of a deck.

4

ATTACH STRINGERS TO PAD AND DECK

Fasten the stringers to a 1×6 cleat attached to the concrete pad or sidewalk. Attach the cleat to concrete with threaded studs (see page 80). Install the stringers in joist hangers attached to the deck.

5

INSTALL END STRIP

Attach the 1½-inch-wide strip to the ends of the stringers with the widest face against the stringers. Drill pilot holes for the fasteners to prevent splitting.

6

INSTALL TREADS

Fasten the first tread with an overhang of about 1 inch. Install the remaining treads with ⅛-inch gaps between them.

7

POUR CONCRETE TRANSITION

Smooth concrete poured to make a transition from the ramp to the pad or sidewalk. Apply a bonding agent over existing concrete. Make sure concrete fills the space under the lip of the final tread.

Railings

ore than any other design element, it's the railing that sets the style of a deck. Most decks and stairs need a railing.

Choose a railing style that complements your house, deck, and landscape, and make this decision before you install decking—some railing posts must be attached before the decking goes down. By the time you're ready to install the railing, your deck is almost completed, and you might be tempted to work quickly. Resist that urge and work carefully—mistakes

here will show up more dramatically than anywhere else in the structure.

There are many ways of attaching a railing to a deck structure, but the most common is to fasten posts to the perimeter joists and hang the railings between them. Here's where you can get creative. You can install milled balusters or plain ones, vertical balusters or intricate designs of your own making, wood or plastic panels, or the open weave of lattice work. Almost anything goes in railing style—except for those restrictions placed on your creativity by local building codes. Most codes require a deck with

Chapter 8 highlights

RAILING TIPS
Whether you need some alternative ideas about post design, or tips on putting up railings, you'll find them here.

144

INSTALLING RAILINGS
Railings are the most visible aspect of a deck. This section illustrates methods that apply to a variety of different styles.

148

RAILINGS FOR ANGLED STAIRS
Angled stairs add a nice touch to a rectangular deck design and help provide an outlet into the rest of the landscape.

154

RAILING WITH COATED METAL BALUSTERS
This is just one of many examples of how alternative materials can be worked into successful railing designs.

156

INSTALLING A SYNTHETIC RAILING SYSTEM
If you're installing synthetic decking, you'll want your railing to blend in with the overall look of your materials. Synthetic railings require some special installation techniques.

159

more than two steps to have a railing, and second-story decks need a 42-inch railing. Balusters must be spaced close enough together so that a 4-inch sphere cannot pass through. Pay particular attention to spacing for milled balusters. In most cases balusters have to run vertically; most codes do not allow horizontal balusters because children can use them as a ladder to climb over the railing. Always check with your local building code officials before you start designing and building.

Railing tips

ESTABLISH HEIGHT AT CORNERS
To mark throughout at the correct height for the railing, use a water level to establish the line on corner posts. Then install posts and snap a chalkline at the marks.

GANG POSTS FOR NOTCHING
Cut identically spaced notches in posts by clamping them together, called ganging, before cutting. Ganging is quicker than cutting notches one at a time. Line up the post ends before clamping them.

You may want to install a small support block for longer railing spans.

CLOSER LOOK

CAP RAIL OR PROTRUDING POSTS
Post tops can be covered by a cap rail (near right), which makes a smooth, uninterrupted line around the deck. Cap rails are a common treatment but not the only one. Another option is to let post tops protrude above the top rail (far right). Milled posts or decorative caps or finials are often used in this style. Milled posts usually aren't long enough to be through posts (page 146). In that case use pressure-treated lumber and mill your own design.

NOTCHED CORNER POST

Install a notched post at a corner (above, left) to save the cost and time of installing a post on each side of the corner. Cutting this type of notch is more complicated than notches cut across the face of a post. To make your style consistent throughout, attach your rails in a notch at the top of the post (above, right). Install the rails with mitered corners. Drill pilot holes and drive deck screws at an angle to fasten the rails into the notch.

TWO-POST CORNER

You can attach one post on each side of a deck corner when installing posts without notches. Space the posts about a baluster's width apart. Fasten the rails to the inner post faces. Use a butt joint or a mitered joint where the rails meet.

MITER CUTS IMPROVE LOOK

You can dress up even the least expensive materials with just a few cuts. Here the balusters and post have been run through a tablesaw to create the mitered ends.

2× cleat adds support.

Header

Interior joist

Carriage bolt

THROUGH POSTS

Through posts extend from the footings above the deck surface to support railings or overheads. Such support is needed for large, heavy overhead structures, but through posts are often employed in designs without overheads.

Most often installed with the perimeter joists fastened on their outside faces, through posts require you to cut notches in the decking. Cut them about ⅛ inch wider to allow drainage. Add perpendicular blocking to keep the post from tilting under stress.

CLOSER LOOK

SCARF JOINT ADDS STRENGTH WHERE NEEDED
Join two rail pieces that attach to the face of a post with a scarf joint (near right) for a stronger joint than a butt joint. Cut opposing 45-degree bevels in the ends of the rail pieces. Center the joint on the post face. The length of a 45-degree bevel cut in a 2¥ board is 1½ inches. Use this measurement when you figure necessary rail lengths. Drill pilot holes and drive fasteners at an angle through the joint to attach the rail pieces. Use a butt joint between rail pieces installed in a notch because the notch provides strong support. Make the outer face of each rail flush with a perimeter joist face if balusters will be attached to the perimeter joists (far right). For example, fasten rails to inner faces of posts installed without notches for the balusters to be vertical.

8

RAILINGS

RAILING REINFORCEMENTS

Strengthen railing posts by installing additional framing, especially on notched posts that support an overhead. For posts on a header, add 2× blocking between the joists. This creates a thicker base for the carriage bolts. On rim joists add blocking between the interior joists to reduce flexing. The strongest support of all is achieved by using a steel anchor, which transfers any lateral stress to the interior joist.

 DESIGN TIP

CUSTOMIZE YOUR RAILINGS

It doesn't take much to make a fancy railing. You can buy premilled decorative spindles from your home center. They are best installed in a rabbet (or groove) cut in the center of the top and bottom rails. Lattice is less expensive and installs between 1× stops nailed to the inside faces of the posts. Both materials create a stylish alternative to standard 2×2 balusters.

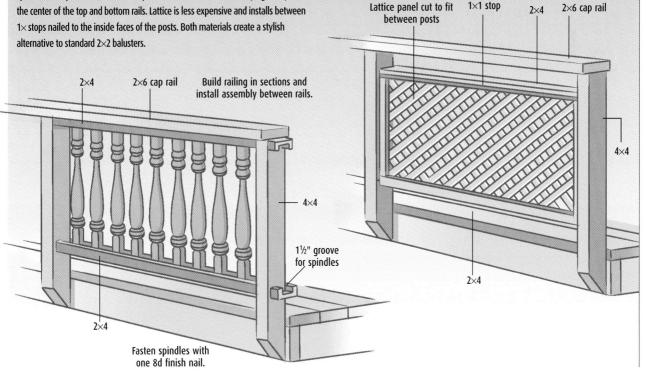

2×4   2×6 cap rail   Build railing in sections and install assembly between rails.

4×4

1½" groove for spindles

2×4

Fasten spindles with one 8d finish nail.

Lattice panel cut to fit between posts   1×1 stop   2×4   2×6 cap rail

4×4

2×4

Installing railings

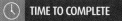
Building codes vary, but most require a railing on decks more than 30 inches above the ground. (Some are more stringent, requiring a railing on any deck more than two steps above grade.) A railing height requirement of 36 inches is common.

Railing posts can be attached to the outer face of the perimeter joists, or can be through posts supported by the footings. You can install railing in notched or unnotched posts, but notches are required if the decking overhangs the perimeter joists.

Use any railing style that meets code. Spacing between balusters and between lower rails and decking can be no more than 4 inches in order to prohibit a child from getting through or stuck between the balusters. Plan spacing carefully if you choose balusters with decorative profiles because uneven surfaces may create larger spaces.

Here's how to calculate the number of balusters you'll need between the posts, assuming 1½-inch balusters and a minimum spacing of 3¾ inches:

1. Add the width of a baluster (i.e.: 1½ inches) to the desired spacing. (1½" + 3¾" = 5¼")
2. Divide this into the total distance between posts. (70" ÷ 5¼" or 5.25" = 13.34)
3. Round to the nearest whole number to find the number of balusters—13 for the example.
4. Multiply this by the width of one baluster. (13 × 1½" = 19½")
5. Subtract this from the total distance between posts. (70" − 19½" = 50½")
6. Add 1 to the number of balusters to find the number of spacings. (In the example, 13 + 1 = 14)
7. Divide this into the remainder from Step 5 to find the actual spacing measurement between balusters. (50½" or 50.5" ÷ 14 = 3.6 or 3⅝")
8. With rounding the last space may be slightly different. This will not be noticeable. (In the example, spacing the balusters 3⅝ inches apart means the last space will actually be about 3½ inches.)

1

MEASURE RAILING RUN
Measure the exact dimension of each railing run. A railing run is a straight section of railing uninterrupted by stairs or other changes in direction. Calculate the number and location of posts and the gap between balusters for each run.

2 **ATTACH POSTS**

Plumb and attach each post with two carriage bolts or lag screws. Stagger the fasteners on both sides of the center of the post to prevent splitting. Cut notches in posts before attaching, if necessary for the railing style. Make notches for rails the same depth as the notches on the rim joist.

3 **FASTEN RAILS TO POSTS**

Fasten each rail to the posts. Drill pilot holes for fasteners at the ends of each rail to prevent splitting.

4 **MARK POST FOR STAIR STRINGER**

Mark the slanted top shoulder of a notch for a post that will attach to a stair stringer. Plumb the post against the stringer at its correct height before marking. Cut the notch and install the post. Position one post at each end of a stair run. Install additional posts for long stair runs or to match the railing design.

5 **SET STAIR RAILING HEIGHT**

Mark the location for the upper edge of the top rail or for trimming the post top, depending on the railing style. Lay a long straight 2×4 across the stair treads. Measure to the railing height from the bottom edge of the 2×4 at each post to mark the top edge of a stair railing.

8

RAILINGS

6 **LAY OUT NOTCHES FOR RAILING**

Mark the notches for each stair rail in the posts. Hold or clamp the rails in position against the posts.

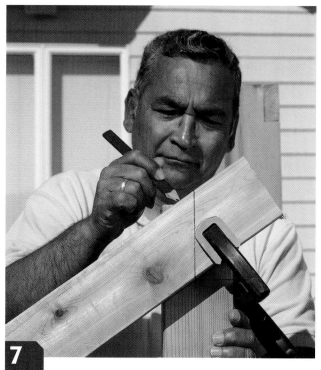

7 **MARK CUTTING LINE AT END**

Mark cutting lines on the end of the stair rail. End the rail in the center of the post if it meets a deck rail at the post. Also mark the stair rail notch location on the post. The post shown is trimmed to proper height.

CLOSER LOOK

STRONG JOINTS DON'T COME EASY

One method to make a joint between a stair rail and a deck rail is to center the joint in a notch in the post (near right). This makes a very strong joint; however, the complex shape of the notch makes it more complicated to cut. Notice how the end of the stair rail must be trimmed to make it meet with the square end of the deck rail. The other option is to attach only the deck rail in a straight notch. The straight notch is easier to cut, but the stair rail must be toenailed to the end of the deck rail (far right). Matching angles are cut in the ends of the stair and deck rails and do not create as strong a joint as the centered rail.

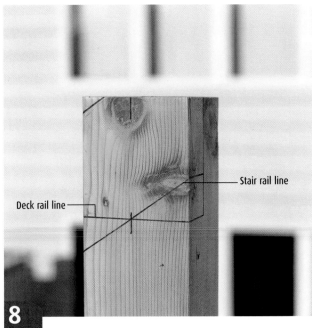

8
LAY OUT NOTCH WHERE RAILS MEET

Mark the notch location for a deck rail that meets a stair rail at a post. The top of a post where stair rail and deck rail meet will be level with other posts for the deck railing.

Stair rail line
Deck rail line

9
CUT NOTCH IN POST

Cut the notch in the post. Remove as much of the notch as possible with a circular saw (page 90). Then finish removing waste material with a chisel.

10
MARK ANGLE ON RAILS

Mark the intersecting angle between the stair rail and deck rail. Place the edge of the deck rail on the decking with one end protruding over the stairs. Lay the stair rail on edge on the treads to cross the deck rail. Mark both edges on both rails where they cross. Connect the marks across the face of each rail. Align a power mitersaw blade with a marked line and cut each rail to length.

🔖 **WORK SMARTER**

CUT IT TWICE TO TEST BLADE ANGLE

Make the first cut for an unknown angle about ⅛ inch from the marked line. This will determine whether the power mitersaw blade is aligned correctly. Adjust the blade angle if there is an uneven space between the line and the kerf. Then make the final cut. Making the first cut a short distance away from the line prevents cutting a rail too short with a misaligned blade.

11 ATTACH RAILS

Attach the stair rails to the posts. Drill pilot holes at the ends of each rail to prevent splitting.

12 INSTALL BALUSTERS

Install each baluster with two fasteners at each end. Clamp several balusters to the rails at the spacing you used earlier—to make sure the spacing looks right. If it doesn't, reclamp the balusters and recalculate their number. Cut a spacer long enough to span between rails and as wide as the gap between balusters. Check plumb every fourth baluster.

DESIGN TIP

RAILING DESIGN

Make a unique focal point in a railing with a special baluster design, such as this simple sunburst pattern. Special designs have to comply with the maximum allowable space between balusters.

Scarf joint

45°

13 ATTACH CAP RAIL

Attach 2×6 cap rail across the tops of the posts and balusters. Join sections over a post and with a scarf joint. Drive two fasteners into posts. Drive one fastener every 12–16 inches between posts into rails and balusters.

8

RAILINGS

14 MITER RAIL ENDS

Miter the ends of the cap rail and drive fasteners both through the corners and into the corner posts.

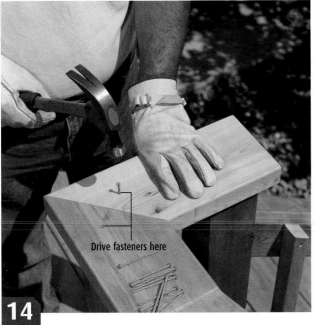

15 MARK STAIR RAIL

Rough-cut a 2×6 a few inches longer than the finished length of the stair rail and hold or clamp it against the upper stair rail where it meets the post. Mark the bevel in the top end and cut it.

16 NAIL RAIL TO POST

Drive fasteners at an angle through the beveled end of the cap rail and into the post. Drill pilot holes to prevent splitting.

17 ADD A HANDHOLD

Attach a graspable handrail inside the stair railing, if necessary. Use brass, galvanized, or other rust-resistant hardware. Sand any sharp edges on the handrail.

18 **RAILING RETURN**

To fasten a handrail return, miter the ends of the handrail stock at 45 degrees. Test-fit the pieces before attaching them.

🎨 **DESIGN TIP**

INSTALLING CAP RAILS

Install upper and lower rails and the cap rail between post faces if post tops protrude above rails in the railing design. Attach the rails to post faces with toenailed screws. Or install rails on small metal angle brackets (see page 157).

8 RAILINGS

Railings for angled stairs

1 **INSTALL STARTING POST**

Install a stair railing post at the top end of an angled stair stringer. Make a space between the post and the deck rail post no wider than the spacing between balusters. Also install the stair railing post at the bottom end of the stringer.

2 **MARK ANGLES**

Mark the angle for trimming each stair rail. Measure and mark locations for rail height (page 149). Temporarily position each stair rail board against the stair rail posts at the marks to mark the trimming line at each end of the board.

3 CUT MITERS ON ENDS

Cut the miter at both ends of each stair rail (see "Work Smarter" on page 151).

4 COMPLETE RAILING

Install the stair rails, balusters, and cap rail following the methods used on the deck railing.

 CLOSER LOOK

CUTTING COMPOUND MITERS

Attaching an angled stair rail to the face of a post requires cutting a compound miter in the stair rail. A compound miter is one that has both a bevel and a miter—it angles in two directions at once. It's easiest to cut a compound miter with a compound mitersaw (right). Because it often takes trial and error to make a tight fit between rail and post, start with the railing 1 foot longer than necessary. Cut the compound miter first. When that fits correctly, make a square cut at the other end to trim the rail to its final length.

Miter cut

Bevel cut

Railing with coated metal balusters

1 **ATTACH POSTS**

Attach railing posts following the method shown on page 149. Measure and cut pairs of 2×4 rails to fit between each run of railing.

2 **LAY OUT LOCATIONS**

Compute the spacing for the metal balusters (page 148) and mark a story pole at this spacing. Clamp as many rails together as possible (with their ends flush), and mark the baluster locations on the rails from the story pole. Place the story pole so the holes are centered and the end holes are at least 1½ inches from the rail ends. Use a speed square or framing square to mark locations accurately.

3 **BORE HOLES**

Using a Forstner bit (it makes flat-bottomed holes), drill a ¾-inch hole to a depth of ¾ inch at each mark. Use a portable drill guide to make holes consistently vertical.

⊙ **TOOL SAVVY**

DRILL THE RIGHT HOLE

Where appearance is important, drill holes with a Forstner bit. This bit cuts a hole with a crisp edge and flat bottom. A spade bit usually cuts a hole with a more ragged edge. Use a spade bit when drilling holes for carriage bolts and lag screws.

4
INSERT BALUSTERS IN BOTTOM RAIL
Insert a baluster in each hole in the bottom rail after applying a small amount of silicone caulk in each hole. The caulk helps prevent moisture penetration. **Wear gloves when using silicone.**

5
PUT ON TOP RAIL
Caulk the holes in the top rail and slide a 1×4 under the top of the balusters. Brace the bottom rail to keep it from moving, and fit the top rail over the ends of the balusters. Stand the assembly upright. Hammer against a scrap wood block placed on the top rail to completely seat both ends of the balusters in the rails.

6
INSTALL ASSEMBLED RAILINGS
Install each rail assembly between the appropriate posts.

📖 WORK SMARTER

STRONG BRACKETS
Small angle brackets make a strong and easy connection when attaching rails between post faces. Fasten the brackets to the post faces at the proper heights. Position one bracket underneath each rail end location. Set the rails onto the brackets. Drive screws through the brackets into the rails and toenail a screw through the top edge of each rail.

7

INSTALL CAP RAIL

Attach the cap rail over the top rail. Join cap rail pieces with a scarf joint centered over a post (page 152). Make 45-degree miter joints at the corners (page 153).

8

DRILL STAIR RAILS ON STAIRS

Drill holes for stair rail balusters with the rails resting on the stair treads. Cut the rails to length with the ends trimmed at the proper angle. Turn the top rail 180 degrees and flip it upside down before clamping the rails together. Mark hole locations 5½ inches on center. (Mark the other edge of the story pole.) Use a level to plumb the portable drill guide, if necessary.

 DESIGN TIP

9

ASSEMBLE AND INSTALL STAIR RAILINGS

Assemble and install the stair rail sections with the same methods used for the deck railing.

RAILING APPEAL

Centerpieces, in various styles and matching colors, attach to metal balusters easily with screws provided by the manufacturer. Finials for post tops also are available.

Installing a synthetic railing system

PROJECT DETAILS

SKILLS: Measuring and cutting lumber, driving fasteners
PROJECT: Installing a synthetic railing on a 16×12-foot deck

TIME TO COMPLETE

EXPERIENCED: 15 hrs.
HANDY: 17 hrs.
NOVICE: 20 hrs.

STUFF YOU'LL NEED

TOOLS: Tape measure, level, clamp, chisel, hammer, power mitersaw, drill
MATERIALS: Synthetic railing materials, fasteners

Almost every manufacturer of synthetic decking material makes a corresponding synthetic railing system—some in more than one style. The components consist of the pieces normally associated with railings—all the parts needed to complete your deck in a consistent style. Some come with railing posts, others with a sleeve that is made to slip over the post so its appearance matches that of the rest of the system.

The system shown here is only one of many and will give you a general idea of the steps involved. Consult the manufacturer's directions when putting up your railing.

1

INSTALL POSTS

Install pressure-treated railing posts or synthetic posts if supplied by the manufacturer, spacing the posts according to the manufacturer's instructions. Slide the post skirts over the posts and let them rest on the deck.

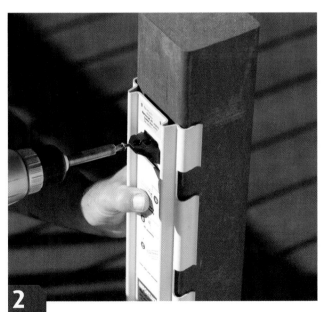

2

ATTACH BRACKETS TO POSTS

Insert two railing brackets into the assembly tool and push the tool on the interior faces of the post sleeves. Attach the brackets to the posts with the screws provided. Remove the tool and repeat the procedure on every post. If your railing does not come with an assembly tool, attach the brackets at the positions specified by the manufacturer.

3

INSTALL BALUSTERS

Lay the assembly tool face up and place balusters in the slots. Insert all balusters into the channel on the top rail, making sure that the distance from the end of the top rail and the first baluster are equal on both ends. Fasten the balusters with predrilled screws through the bottom lip of the top rail.

4   **PUT ON BOTTOM RAIL**

Move the spacing tool to the bottom of the balusters and slide the bottom rail against them, with the end spacing equal to that of the top rail.

5   **FASTEN BALUSTERS**

Fasten the balusters to the bottom rail by driving predrilled screws through the underside of the rail.

6   **CUT SUPPORT BLOCKS**

Cut support blocks to the manufacturer's specifications from the balusters with a power mitersaw.

7   **INSTALL SUPPORT BLOCKS**

Fasten the support blocks with predrilled screws driven through the lip of the bottom rail.

8

INSTALL RAILING SECTION

Take the complete railing section and place it between the posts, keeping it raised slightly above the mounting brackets.

9

ATTACH RAIL TO BRACKETS

Let the railing section down on the brackets. Fasten it to the top rail by driving a screw through the holes in the mounting bracket into the railing.

10

ATTACH BOTTOM RAIL

Fasten the bottom rail by driving a screw through the top of the rail into the bracket. Repeat the process for the remaining sections.

11

FINISH WITH POST CAPS

Finish the railing by attaching the post caps according to the manufacturer's instructions. Some are made to snap into the post skirt, others require the application of construction adhesive.

STYLE AND DURABILITY

The handsome railing matches the decking to create a unified look. The railing is sturdy and the composite materials will not rot, so it will retain its strength.

Building deck accessories

lthough any of the designs and techniques shown in the earlier sections of this book will result in a long-lasting, attractive deck, there is almost no aspect of a deck that cannot be altered to make it more stylish or useful. Most of these alternatives, such as built-in benches, privacy screens, and arbors, require installation during deck building. Others, like some types of low-voltage lighting, can be added later, after you've used the deck for a while and determined what you need. Installing lighting for a raised deck, for example, often is easier after the deck is built.

Whatever alterations or amenities you carry out, be sure to include them in your plans from the start. You can add an overhead structure on some decks after you've built them, but you'll want to beef up the footings for the extra weight during the initial construction of the deck, particularly if heftier footings are required by your local codes.

Chapter 9 highlights

ATTACHING SKIRTING AND FASCIA
Skirting and fascia are just two ways to dress up the appearance of a deck.

164

BUILDING BENCHES
Benches add seating and can be used to help define different areas of use on different areas of the deck.

166

BUILDING A PRIVACY SCREEN
Decks are not structures for public display. You'll need some privacy, and this screen is an easy way to get it.

169

BUILDING AN OVERHEAD STRUCTURE
The term "overhead structure" applies to arbors, pergolas, and sometimes solid roofs. The construction methods for each of these additions are basically the same.

170

CUTTING A CURVED DECK
Curved decks provide a stylish alternative to the squared corners of rectangular decks. They are remarkably easy to design and build.

173

LOW-VOLTAGE LIGHTING
Low-voltage lighting is inexpensive, easy to install, and adds warmth and safety to your deck.

174

INSTALLING DECKING ON A SLAB
This is an idea that can save you from having to break up that old patio slab that's been sitting out there unused for years.

175

BUILDING A FLOATING-FOUNDATION DECK
Floating foundations don't require you to dig and pour footings. With this novel idea, you can put up a simple deck in a day.

176

Attaching skirting and fascia

PROJECT DETAILS

SKILLS: Measuring and cutting lumber and lattice, driving fasteners
PROJECT: Attaching skirting and fascia to a 16×12-foot deck

TIME TO COMPLETE

EXPERIENCED: 1 hr.
HANDY: 1.5 hrs.
NOVICE: 2 hrs.

STUFF YOU'LL NEED

TOOLS: Tape measure, straightedge, small sledge, hammer, nail set, circular saw, drill
MATERIALS: Lumber, lattice, rebar, fasteners, sliding bolts or hook-and-eye hardware

Skirting and fascia are both excellent devices for covering things up—skirting for the empty and unattractive underside of a deck, and fascia for less expensive framing lumber.

You have several material choices when it comes to installing skirting. You can construct skirts of lattice or use panels made from siding material. Lattice is cheaper by far and can be quite attractive, especially if you use the same wood species you use on your railings, or plant climbing plants after you've put up the panels. You may want to back lattice with netting to prevent small animals from getting under your deck, especially if you use the space for storage. Install hinged or lift-away panels in the skirting to give you access to storage areas.

One of the primary uses of fascia is to add a trimmed-out appearance, covering pressure-treated lumber in the framing. Cut fascia from the same wood used for the railing, such as cedar or redwood. Fascia also may be installed to cover the ends of decking boards; however, this method may trap moisture and hasten wood deterioration in damp climates.

2×4 rails

1

INSTALL RAILS

Install 2×4 rails between posts so you have a nailing surface for the skirting. Cut lattice to size with a circular saw guided by a long straightedge. Attach the skirting with short deck screws after drilling pilot holes to prevent splitting. Trim the edges with 1× stock for a more finished look.

9

BUILDING DECK ACCESSORIES

2

FRAME ACCESS OPENINGS

Frame storage access panels by first adding pressure-treated 4×4s across the bottom of the open area. Predrill the 4×4s for rebar and drive 18-inch lengths of rebar through them to hold them in place.

1×
lumber

3

MAKE ACCESS PANELS

Make the panels by framing lattice with 1× trim. Hinges aren't necessary. Just install sliding bolts or hook-and-eye hardware to hold the panel in place. Use brass or other rust-resistant hardware.

CLOSER LOOK

ATTACHING FASCIA

Fasten fascia to framing with galvanized finish nails (near right). Deck screws aren't necessary, and finishing nails are less noticeable. Measure, cut, and install fascia with mitered ends around corners (far right). Drive nails through the mitered joint from both directions to keep the joint tight. Use a nail set to drive nailheads flush with the wood surface to prevent the hammer from dimpling the fascia.

Building benches

Deck benches can be either freestanding or built in. The advantage of freestanding benches is that you can move them anywhere you need additional seating. Built-in benches are fastened to joists, and they make a nice addition at the perimeter of a low-level deck that doesn't require a railing. The benches help define the edge of the deck.

On higher decks be careful where you place freestanding benches so children don't use them to climb over a railing. On a deck that requires a railing, the railing must extend 36 inches above the top of the bench. To gain storage, enclose the area beneath a bench seat.

Build benches from 2× lumber for stability. Typical seat height for a bench is 15 to18 inches. Seat depth is usually at least 15 inches but may be as much as 30 inches. The bench projects beginning on this page are 5 feet long. The seats are 18 inches high and 17 inches deep. Use dimensions that suit your needs or pattern your bench after one you've seen elsewhere. Benches complement your deck best when made from the same type of wood used for the decking and railing. To provide a smooth seating surface, sand all surfaces and round over sharp corners and edges with a palm sander.

Building a freestanding bench

1

MAKE UPPER PEDESTAL
Mark the layout for the upper pedestal (see Step 4 photo) on a 16-inch 4×4. Space notches for the legs 1½ inches apart. Mark the angles on each end 1 inch from the outer shoulders of the notches. Using a circular saw, cut notches 3½ inches wide and 1½ inches deep (page 90). Remove waste material with a chisel.

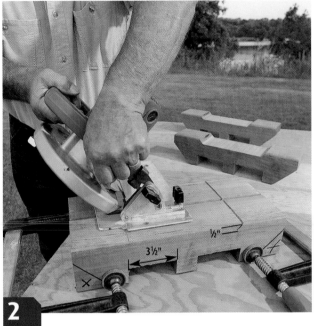

2 CUT LOWER PEDESTAL

Notch the lower pedestal to accommodate the legs. Then cut the the angled shoulder at both ends of the pedestal.

3 ATTACH LEGS

Cut the legs to length (12½ inches). Install one leg in each of the lower pedestals with three screws through the pedestal into the leg. Attach the 2×6 spreader to the inside surface of the legs at both ends of the bench. Drive three deck screws at each end. Fasten the spreader flush with the outer face of each leg.

4 BUILD SEAT

Fasten the rails to the undersides of the 2×6 seat boards with 2½-inch-long deck screws. Position the outer faces of the rails 4½ inches from the board ends. Space the seat boards with a ¼-inch gap between them.

5 INSTALL SEAT

Drive screws through the 2×2 rails into the upper pedestals. Position the seat on the pedestals for a ½-inch overhang on each long side. Rail positions create 1-inch overhangs at the ends.

Building a built-in bench

DESIGN TIP

BUILT-IN BENCH PERPENDICULAR TO JOISTS

Bolt or screw a 2×10 leg on one side of a joist at each end of the bench location. Space legs no more than four 16-inch-on-center joists apart. Cut and install rails and seat as shown in a parallel joist installation. Add blocking between joists to prevent the bench from rocking.

ADD A BORDER OF COLOR

Make railing planters to add floral color to your deck. Build them from 1× lumber of the same type of wood used on the deck. Space the sides to fit over the cap rail. Make butt joints between side, end, and bottom pieces. Fasten pieces together with deck screws. Drill several ½-inch-diameter drain holes in the bottom and attach small feet to the underside to provide air circulation.

BUILT-IN BENCH PARALLEL TO JOISTS

Bolt a 2×10 leg on both sides of the joist at each end of the bench location. Add blocking between joists to prevent the bench from rocking. Space the inside edges of the legs 30 inches apart for a 5-foot-long bench. Miter the lower corners of the 16-inch 2×6 or 2×8 rails and fasten them across the edges of each pair of legs (above, left). Make the top edge of a rail flush with the ends of the legs. Attach 2×6 seat boards, leaving a ¼-inch gap between them. Drive screws through additional rails installed on the underside of the boards (above, right) as shown on page 167. Attach cleats to the legs to support the decking.

Building a privacy screen

Depending on the height and length of your privacy screen, local codes may require that at least the end posts are through posts—supported by footings. Posts supporting a high screen may require permanent bracing.

You can use a variety of materials for the screen panels. Use lattice if some sun and air movement are desired. Train a vining plant on the lattice for greater privacy. Install solid material such as tinted plastic or vertical or horizontal 1× stock for greater privacy and as a windbreak.

1 ATTACH RAILS TO POSTS
Install 2×4 rails across the tops of the posts. Attach flat 2×4 rails for the lower framing between the posts, spacing them 3 inches above decking.

2 INSTALL STOPS ON ONE SIDE
Attach ⁵⁄₄ mitered stops to the posts and the 2×4 framing, centering them with a chalk line. Install the stops on one side of the frame only.

3 INSTALL PANELS
Cut lattice frames to fit the openings and set them (but don't nail them) in the frames against the ⁵⁄₄ stops. Then attach the stops on the other side of the lattice panels.

Building an overhead structure

PROJECT DETAILS

SKILLS: Measuring and cutting lumber, driving fasteners
PROJECT: Building a pergola

TIME TO COMPLETE

EXPERIENCED: 6 hrs.
HANDY: 8 hrs.
NOVICE: 10 hrs.

STUFF YOU'LL NEED

TOOLS: Tape measure, layout square, level, water level, hammer, drill, miter gauge, circular saw, power mitersaw
MATERIALS: Lumber, fasteners, adjustable post anchors, adjustable post caps, rafter ties

B uild a pergola with the same basic building methods used in deck building. Spacing of structural framing usually can be greater because of the lighter load—check with local code. The number of cover pieces depends on how much shade you desire. Install beams at different heights to make a sloping arbor roof. Make temporary braces from plywood weighted with concrete blocks. In some areas arbors are considered building structures. Check with local building officials to make sure the arbor you have planned meets code.

1 INSTALL POST BASES
Install 4×4 posts in metal half bases made for fastening posts to a wooden structure. Attach the half bases to the decking after installing the proper blocking (see page 171).

2 INSTALL BEAMS
Attach doubled 2×8 beams to the post tops with adjustable post caps. Install beams on the long sides of the pergola. Brace the posts with sections of ¾-inch plywood.

3 ADD BRACING
Fasten permanent 2×6 gussets to strengthen the frame. Cut curves or other designs in the gussets to make them more decorative and to match the style of the deck.

4

INSTALL RAFTERS

Install 2×6 rafters across the beams, fastening them with rafter ties and spacing them on 16-inch centers. Miter the rafter ends to match the beam ends before installing.

5

ATTACH CEILING SLATS

Install gussets on the remaining corners, and attach 2×2 ceiling slats with deck screws. Cut miters in the ends of the slats before installing.

6

TRIM AROUND POST BASES

Nail mitered 1× trim to cover the post bases, using galvanized finish nails. Drill pilot holes to prevent splitting.

CLOSER LOOK

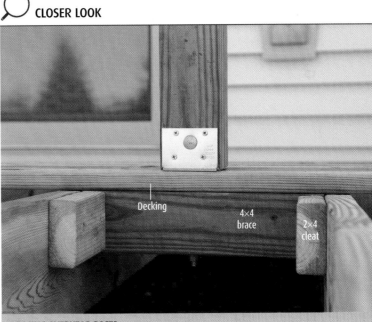

Decking

4×4 brace

2×4 cleat

BRACING OVERHEAD POSTS

When you are installing posts on a decking surface and not to the rim joists, support the post with the blocking shown here. Attach the post base with a machine bolt. Mount the posts after installing the decking board that covers the 4×4 brace, but before the adjacent board. This allows you to reach the nut on the bottom of the bolt.

CLOSER LOOK

ATTACHING A STRUCTURE TO A HOUSE

One side of an overhead structure may be the wall of a house. Install a ledger board at the appropriate height the same way you did to build the deck. Attach one end of the rafters to the ledger board with joist hangers. Use a bevel gauge to determine the trimming angle for rafters that slope from the ledger (near left). Trim the end of each rafter and attach with a skewable joist hanger (far right).

Lattice-roofed shelter

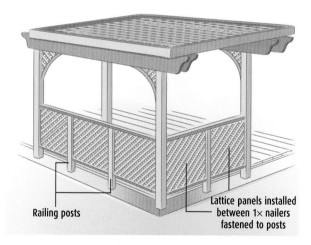

Railing posts

Lattice panels installed between 1× nailers fastened to posts

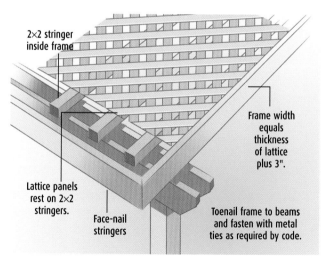

2×2 stringer inside frame

Lattice panels rest on 2×2 stringers.

Face-nail stringers

Frame width equals thickness of lattice plus 3".

Toenail frame to beams and fasten with metal ties as required by code.

Here's a great way to incorporate lattice into an overhead design to create a small but cozy getaway deck. The framed lattice roof offers plenty of shade, and lattice panels in the railings increase privacy and visually tie the design together. Lattice comes in two thicknesses—¼ inch and ¾ inch. The thicker stock resists warping.

For a small arbor, you can build the roof frame, hoist it with a helper or two, and fasten it to the rafters. On a large structure, miter the corners of the frame and toenail the sides to the beams. Then fasten the ends of the frame to the sides. Cut 2×2 stringers to fit inside the frame and face-nail them to the frame with their bottom edges on the beams. Then cut the lattice panels and fasten them.

Cutting a curved deck

1

SCRIBE THE ARC ON THE JOISTS

Make a framing scribe from a piece of ½-inch plywood and a 1×4. Fasten the plywood on the joists over the center point of the curve. Mark the center point on the plywood and fasten a 1×4 scribe with one nail through a predrilled hole in the center of the 1×4. Measure from the nail out to the end of the 1×4 and cut it to the radius of the curve. Move the end of the scribe from one joist to the next, marking each with the angle at which the 1×4 crosses it.

2

Angle of intersection with framing scribe

DRAW CUTTING LINES

Using a layout square, darken the marks on the top of the joists and extend the ends of the marks down both sides of the joists (so you can monitor the angle while you're cutting it).

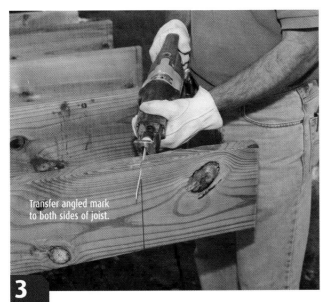

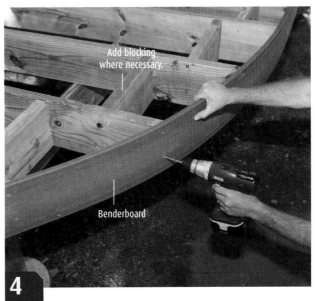

3

Transfer angled mark to both sides of joist.

CUT ENDS OF JOISTS

Line up a reciprocating saw on the angled mark and cut the joist, making sure the blade does not wander away from either line. Have a helper hold the end of a tape measure on the first cut joist and measure the circumference of the arc from that point to the last cut joist. If your tape measure won't conform to the curve around the joists, use mason's line.

4

Add blocking where necessary.

Benderboard

INSTALL BENDERBOARD

Cut benderboard or a 1× board the same width as the joists a little longer than the length of the arc. If you use a 1× board, saw kerfs every ½ inch halfway through the board on the back so the board will bend. Fasten it to the joists and trim it to fit. Add blocking where necessary. Mark the curve on each piece of decking from the underside, then trim it to fit with a jigsaw.

Low-voltage lighting

ow-voltage lighting is available in ready-to-install kits and as individual lights. Surface-mounted lights are easier to install than recessed lights, but you can create a more finished look with recessed lights. Spend some time looking at the outdoor lighting options available and determine the effect you want to create with outdoor lights. Low-voltage lighting installations usually aren't covered by local code because low voltage isn't considered dangerous. The only regular voltage necessary is a GFCI receptacle to plug in the low-voltage unit. Have an electrician install a GFCI if you're not confident of your electrical skills. Follow the manufacturer's installation directions for the product you purchase. Most units install easily with connections snapping together.

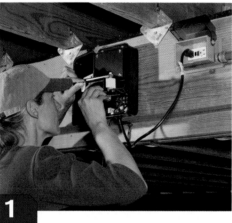

1
INSTALL TRANSFORMER
Connect the low-voltage circuit wires to the transformer terminals. Attach the low-voltage lighting system transformer near a GFCI receptacle. Install the GFCI in an exterior-rated electrical box designed for permanent plug-in use.

2
ROUTE WIRES ALONG FRAMING
Fasten circuit wires to deck framing with exterior-rated cable staples. Route wires on the underside of the deck, under railings, or on the back sides of posts as much as possible.

3
DRILL HOLES FOR WIRES
Run wires through holes drilled inside stairs or other covered locations. Or conceal holes in the seams where decking butts against posts or other framing.

4
INSTALL LIGHT FIXTURES
Insert recessed light units into holes cut in stair risers, perimeter joists, or railing. Position lights to best illuminate stairs and other passageways.

Installing decking on a slab

I f you're plagued with an old drab concrete slab in your backyard, you can upgrade it with decking.

If the slab is relatively level and structurally sound (that is, it won't break up after you've decked it), you can make the space attractive and useable by transforming it into a ground-level deck.

The project centers on sleepers (2×4s fastened flat to the slab), which you can attach with masonry nails or with a power-actuated tool. This tool makes a lot of noise, but what it also makes is quick work out of attaching wood to concrete.

Be sure to install the sleepers (pressure-treated, of course) perpendicular to the house to allow rainwater to drain away from the foundation.

1

MARK SLEEPER LOCATIONS ON SLAB

Before you lay the sleepers, snap chalk lines across the slab at 16-inch intervals. Extend the chalk lines up the wall of the house and down the front end of the slab (so you can center the sleepers). Cut the sleepers to length individually (the slab may not be square) and set them out on the center lines. Drive one fastener at each end of each sleeper, keeping the boards on the chalk lines.

2

LEVEL SLEEPERS

Using a 4-foot level, make sure the sleepers are level across the entire surface of the slab. Insert a pair of cedar shims at low spots, taking care not to nudge the sleepers off the center lines.

3

ATTACH SLEEPERS

Fasten the sleepers to the slab through the shims. If a sleeper moves slightly off center, you'll still have plenty of nailing surface on the 2×4 to keep your fastener lines straight.

4

INSTALL DECKING

Using fasteners that will penetrate the decking and sleepers without going through to the concrete (2¾-inch deck screws would be about right), fasten the decking to the sleepers, maintaining at least a ⅛-inch spacing between them.

9

BUILDING DECK ACCESSORIES

Building a floating-foundation deck

PROJECT DETAILS

SKILLS: Measuring and laying out site, setting pier blocks, cutting lumber, building deck

PROJECT: Building a floating-foundation deck

TIME TO COMPLETE

EXPERIENCED: 4 hrs.
HANDY: 6 hrs.
NOVICE: 7 hrs.

STUFF YOU'LL NEED

TOOLS: Tape measure, post level, laser level, hammer, saw, mason's line

MATERIALS: Post piers, posts, lumber for deck

Floating decks, a recent innovation in decking technology, rely on a system of pier blocks to support either joists (for a ground-level structure) or posts and joists (for a raised deck). The preformed concrete piers are blocks designed for such systems, unlike a standard pier block. A 1¾×1¾-inch slot accepts 2× lumber horizontally and the 3¾×3¾-inch socket accepts a 4×4 post. The porous block wicks moisture from the lumber to the ground.

The biggest advantage of this system is that you don't have to dig and pour footing holes. In many situations you can construct a simple deck in one day or a more complicated one in a weekend. The system is engineered to meet building codes, but you should check with your building department to make sure it is accepted in your area.

1 **LAY OUT THE PIERS**
Lay out the site as you would a regular deck, using batterboards and mason's lines as shown on pages 62–64. Mark the site for the spacing required by the manufacturer and set out all the blocks at this spacing. Remove the sod under each block and shovel in about an inch of sand before replacing the block. The sand will make leveling the block easier.

2 **PLACE POSTS**
Cut all the posts slightly longer than their final height, making sure those that will be located on lower ground are long enough. Set the posts in the blocks, rocking the block slightly as you plumb the post. Set up a laser level on a tripod and adjust it so the laser lights the posts at the finished height. Mark each post and cut it with a reciprocating saw and recheck for plumb.

3 INSTALL LEDGER

Cut the ledger to length and fasten it to the house if required by the manufacturer or local codes. Then cut the joists to length and fasten them to the posts with post cap connectors and to the ledger with joist hangers.

4 CONSTRUCT HEADER

Cut the header to length and face-nail it or screw it to the ends of the joists.

5 BRACE THE POSTS

Install crossbraces between the posts if required by the manufacturer or building codes. (Many installations will not require bracing.)

6 INSTALL DECKING

Lay out the decking and install it with the techniques shown on pages 108–123.

Maintenance and repair

t's important to maintain your deck, yet most homeowners don't often think of deck maintenance. Applying a finish on a wood deck ensures that it will look its best—for a while. Climate and normal wear and tear can soon erode both the appearance and integrity of the structure. Climates with the greatest range of weather conditions, of course, increase the amount and frequency of maintenance. Nothing contributes more to the longevity of a deck than a regular maintenance schedule. The key here is "regular." No matter what kind of finish or how much care you've taken in building your deck, you should examine it thoroughly once a year. The examination tips on pages 183–184 will tell you some of the things to look for. Pay close attention to the fasteners. The new pressure-treatment chemicals

Chapter 10 highlights

APPLYING FINISH
Finishes can alter the appearance of the wood dramatically, but more importantly, almost all materials will benefit from some type of protection from the sun and rain.

180

CLEANING A DECK
Regular cleaning of your deck will keep its appearance in tip-top shape and will help minimize deterioration.

182

INSPECTING A DECK
Regular inspection of your deck should be a routine you perform every year.

183

REPAIRING A DECK
Many deck repairs become necessary in the first five years of its construction, but can be accomplished with a minimum of time and effort. Making repairs when problems occur keeps the deck from suffering more significant damage later.

185

TEARING DOWN AN OLD DECK
Just as decks go up in a certain order, tearing an old one down should proceed in its own order too.

186

will corrode fasteners about twice as fast as the old treatments. And when you find a problem, take care of it immediately. If you're not sure about the solution to a problem, call a deck contractor and ask for a consultation.

Applying finish

PROJECT DETAILS

SKILLS: Spraying, brushing, and rolling finish
PROJECT: Applying finish to a 12×16-foot deck

TIME TO COMPLETE

EXPERIENCED: 3 hrs.
HANDY: 4 hrs.
NOVICE: 5 hrs.
(Doesn't include drying time)

STUFF YOU'LL NEED

TOOLS: Finish sprayer, brush, roller and extension handle
MATERIALS: Tarps and masking paper, finish, roller pad

I f your budget won't allow you to purchase cedar, redwood, or one of the more expensive species but you don't like the look of pressure-treated lumber, don't dismay. You can hide or diminish the brownish tint of PT wood by applying outdoor deck stain. You can also use stain when you want to match the color of the deck to the house siding or trim.

Opaque stains provide the best color coverage of the wood. However, they may peel and require frequent reapplication. Semitransparent stains soak deeply into wood fibers and wear well for longer periods, and they allow more of the wood tone and grain to show. Clear sealers or wood preservatives are good choices for cedar and redwood. They provide protection without diminishing the natural beauty of the wood. Choose a finish product containing mildew prevention.

A clear sealer or preservative must have UV inhibitors or sunlight will break it down and affect wood color. Paint is not a good finish choice because traffic areas quickly show wear. It also requires more frequent maintenance.

Apply one thin coat of finish to penetrate and dry completely. Thick layers of finish neither penetrate nor dry completely. The wood should be dry before applying finish. New pressure-treated lumber must dry out completely before finish is applied. Check with the lumber supplier for the proper amount of drying time.

Make sure whatever finish you apply is rated for outdoor use and for a deck surface. Follow the manufacturer's application instructions for best results. And don't spray or paint yourself into a corner.

Use a deck brightener to clean a deck before applying new finish. A brightener removes dirt, mildew, and the top layer of sun-faded wood fibers to restore the natural color of cedar and redwood.

Reapply finish to decks approximately once per year. Harsh climates and heavy deck usage may require reapplication twice per year.

BUYER'S GUIDE

SPRAY-ON SEALER
Use a hand-pumped sprayer or an electric power sprayer to evenly apply clear sealer, stain, or paint. Use an electric sprayer for large deck areas. Follow manufacturer's directions for use and plan to back-roll and back-brush after spraying the finish material. Spray finish on a windless day and cover shrubs and other objects with tarps.

Hand-pumped sprayer

Power sprayer

DESIGN TIP

Solid color stain

Semitransparent stain

Exterior stain

Clear sealer

Untreated

MAKE STAIN SAMPLES

All finishes will alter the color of all woods, even if only slightly. The photos on this page will give you a rough idea of how much certain products change the color of untreated Douglas fir. Nothing in a photo, however, can convey the actual colors of a stain or paint. Always try out a prospective product on a scrap piece of decking or in an inconspicuous spot before applying it to the entire surface.

1

SPRAY ON FINISH

Apply finish material with a sprayer. Use a hand-pumped unit for small deck areas or apply finish on small decks with a roller and brush. Use a roller on decking after spraying to force finish into the wood and to spread out any pooled material. This method is called back-rolling.

2

BRUSH END GRAIN

Use a brush to work the finish into end grain, seams, and gaps between boards. This method is called back-brushing. Back-brush vertical surfaces to remove drips. End grain soaks up finish, and you may need to apply more.

Cleaning a deck

1

SCRAPE OFF LOOSE FINISH

Remove loose paint or opaque stain with a paint scraper. Scrape down damaged areas to bare wood. Then sand each area to feather the edges of remaining finish material down to bare wood.

2

SCRUB THE SURFACE

Use a stiff bristle brush to remove flaking stain or dirt. Don't use a metal-bristle brush on cedar or redwood because the metal bristles may scar the soft wood.

CLOSER LOOK

READY FOR THE SEALER: THE BEAD TEST

Is your deck sealed properly or is it ready for a new coat? Try the bead test to make sure. Sometimes the answer is obvious. Old wood with a dried-out look clearly needs a stiff dose of sealer. But boards that look OK may also be in danger of drying out. So do the following test once or twice a year: Sprinkle a little water on the surface. If the water beads up and does not soak in within two minutes, the board is sealed well enough. If water soaks in within two minutes, apply additional sealer.

3   APPLY CLEANER

Apply a deck brightener product to wood surfaces. Mix the product according to manufacturer's directions. Work the brightener into the wood with a stiff bristle brush, using an extension handle on the brush, if necessary.

4   POWER WASH DECK

Wash the deck surfaces to remove brightener solution and other residue, using a power washer with a fan spray nozzle. The extra pressure of this tool is necessary to adequately clean the deck. Let the deck dry thoroughly before applying new finish. Be careful power washing a cedar deck. Use the low power setting to avoid damaging the wood.

Inspecting a deck

LOOSE BOARDS

Repair loose or damaged decking. Loose fasteners can be driven back in. Replace boards that are severely cupped or deteriorating.

ROT

Poke the tip of a narrow-blade screwdriver into suspect areas. Wood that the tip easily penetrates is rotting.

OVERCUT STRINGERS

Check for overcut notches on open stair stringers. Replace dangerously weak stringers that have overcut notches (note the saw kerfs extending past the notch).

MISALIGNED STRINGERS
Examine stair stringers for misaligned notches and treads, or tread runs less than 10 inches. The stringer shown does not support treads properly.

INCORRECT INSTALLATION
Improperly fastened stringers must be replaced. A slot cut for a standard joist hanger in the top end of the stringer, as shown, has seriously weakened the stringer. Toenailing also is not adequate.

MOISTURE TRAPS
Decking that falls short of framing along a deck perimeter may form a moisture trap. Wood may deteriorate quickly in these spots.

WATER DAMAGE
Examine the ledger for signs of water damage or rot. Presence of either of these usually indicates absent or improperly installed flashing.

BALUSTER SPACING
Measure the spacing between balusters and beneath bottom rails. Gaps greater than 4 inches are a code violation and are potentially dangerous.

MOLD AND MILDEW
Look for mildew or mold on wood surfaces. These generally can be removed with a thorough cleaning (pages 182–183).

Repairing a deck

R epair and maintenance needs for a well-built deck less than 10–15 years old are few. They usually involve resetting some fasteners, replacing a few pieces of decking, cleaning the deck to remove dirt and mildew, or reapplying finish. An older deck, especially one included in a home purchase, may have more problems. Moisture damage or rot in deck framing indicates that it is time for a new deck. One deteriorating joist or post usually indicates that more will soon follow. Replace any deck that has several of the problems shown on pages 183–184.

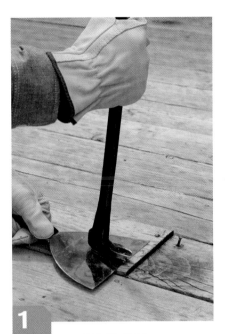 

1

PULL POPPED NAILS
Remove loose or popped nails with a cat's paw (above, left) or pry bar. Protect the board surface with a wide putty knife. Drive long deck screws in place of the nails (above, right). Drill pilot holes and use additional screws if necessary.

2

REMOVE DAMAGED DECKING
Drive the claws of a cat's paw underneath nailheads to pry them out when removing damaged decking (above, left). Use a pry bar to lift out damaged boards (above, center). Protect adjacent boards with a wide putty knife. Cut and install replacement boards. Let a new board overhang at the edge of a deck (above, right); it's quicker and more accurate to trim in place than to trim before installing.

Tearing down an old deck

PROJECT DETAILS

SKILLS: Rough cutting of lumber, lifting of demolition waste
PROJECT: Tearing down a 12×16-foot two-level deck

TIME TO COMPLETE

EXPERIENCED: 3 hrs.
HANDY: 5 hrs.
NOVICE: 8 hrs.

STUFF YOU'LL NEED

TOOLS: Reciprocating saw, circular saw, pry bar, hammer, socket wrench
MATERIALS: Waste container

R eplacing a worn-out or poorly built deck first requires its removal. Make this as simple and quick as possible by cutting apart the deck. Have a refuse hauler drop a large waste container as close to the site as possible. Cut the deck into pieces you can easily carry and place into the container. Tell the hauler what material will be placed in the container. Many municipalities charge extra for pressure-treated lumber. Don't mix yard or household waste with construction refuse.

Work safely while demolishing a deck. Have a helper support long joists, beams, and posts, if necessary. Wear safety glasses and a dust mask. Make certain you have stable footing when operating saws.

Tear down the deck in the sequence shown below. Tear down lower deck levels on multilevel decks first. Wear work gloves to protect your hands from splinters and sharp edges. Wear work boots rather than sneakers or other lightweight shoes. Demolition of a high deck or one on a steep slope is better left to a professional.

Check with local code before you begin demolition. Some codes require leaving part of the original structure if you want to replace an existing deck.

1
CUT RAILINGS
Cut railings into 4- to 6-foot-long sections with a reciprocating saw. Install a blade for fast, rough cuts. Trim balusters attached to perimeter joists at decking level.

2
SAW DECKING
Use a circular saw to cut through decking along both sides of each joist. Snap chalk lines to guide the cuts. Remove stair treads and riser boards with a hammer and pry bar.

3

CUT AWAY STRINGERS

Cut each stringer at the top end with a reciprocating saw. You should be able to pry it off a toe-kick or other fasteners at the bottom end.

4

REMOVE JOISTS

Use a reciprocating saw to cut each joist just inside the joist hangers or other fasteners. Begin each cut at the top edge of a joist.

5

CUT OFF BEAMS

Cut through posts just underneath the beams, using a reciprocating saw. Install a blade long enough to pass completely through the post.

6

REMOVE LEDGER

Use a pry bar to pry the ledger from the house after screws and bolts are unfastened. Also remove old flashing if present. Check for damaged sheathing or framing behind the ledger before installing a new ledger.

A

Access hatch, building, 115
Access panels for storage, 165
Access ramp, building, 139-141
Anatomy of deck, 8
Anchors, masonry, 39
Angle brackets, rails attached with, 157
Angles
  checking, 46
  with compound mitersaw, 49, 155
  marking, tools for, 45
  stair railings, 49, 151, 154-155
Arbors, 170, 172
Augers, power, footings dug with, 70

B

Balusters, 36
  attaching, 146, 152
  calculations for, 148
  coated metal, installing, 156-158
  decorative effects, 145, 147, 152, 158
  synthetic systems, 159-160
Barriers, moisture and vapor, 37
Batterboards, footings laid out with, 62-65, 67
Beams
  building and installing, 93-97
  diagonal, 17, 64, 96
  framing connectors with, 40, 103-104
  notching posts for, 91
  pergola, 170
  removing, 187
  span table, 21
Benches, 10, 14, 34
  building, 166-168
Benderboard, curved deck with, 173
Bevel angles, cutting, 49, 155
Bevel gauge, use of, 45
Biscuit clips, 123
Bits, drill, 43, 156
Blocking between joists, 103, 171
Boards. See also Lumber
Bolts, 39
  J-bolts, 39, 77-78
Box steps on multilevel decks, 113
Bracing
  for pergola, 170, 171
  for posts, 97, 177
  for stringers, 135

Brackets, angle, rails attached with, 157
Brick landings, 83
Brightener, deck, use of, 183
Building codes, 20, 24
  for footings, 71, 81
Building inspectors, 24
Built-in benches, 166, 168

C

Cameras, use of, in site planning, 13
Cap rails, 144
  installing, 152-153, 154, 158
  planters fitting over, 168
Carpenter's level, use of, 44
Cedar grade stamp, 31
Ceiling slats on pergola, 171
Circular saws, 46-48
  squaring, 46
Clamshell diggers, use of, 73
Cleaning, deck, 182-183
Climate control, 11, 13
Clips, synthetic decking installed with, 118-119, 121-123
Closed stringers, 127, 132-133
Codes, building, 20, 24
  for footings, 71, 81
Composite decking, use of, 32, 116-118
  curved, 35, 120
  screws for, 38, 117
Compound mitersaws, use of, 49, 155
Computer-assisted plans, 23
Concrete. See also Footings
  estimating, 25
  ledger installation on, 58-59
  mixing, 74-75
  piers, precast, 37, 81, 176
  reinforcement materials, 77, 82, 84
  tools for, 83
  transition from ramp, 141
Copper-base treatments for PT lumber, 28
Corner, stairs wrapped around, 138
Crosscuts, 46
  marking, 44
Curves, decks with, 173
  synthetic materials for, 35, 120

D

Decking installation, 106-123

clips for, 118-119, 121-123
  diagonal, 115
  lumber for, 25, 28-29, 31
  patterns, 19
  removing, 186
  replacing, 185
  on slab, 175
  synthetic, 32-33, 35, 116-120
  track system for, 123
Defects in lumber, kinds of, 30
Demolition of deck, 186-187
Design and planning considerations, 9-11
  anatomy of deck, 8
  code requirements, 20, 24
  decking patterns, 19
  estimating materials, 25
  plans, drawing, 22-23
  site selection, 12-13
  size of deck, 14
  span calculations, 20-21
  styles, basic, 15-18
Detail drawings, 23
Diagonal beams, 17
  footing locations for, 64
  installing, 96
Diagonal decking, installing, 115
Diagonal joist installations, 17, 100-101
Diagonal stringers, 138
Douglas fir, finishes on, 181
Drawings, plan, 22-23
Drills, power, and drill bits, 43, 156

E

Elevated decks, 9, 15
Elevation drawings, 23
Epoxy, use of, 59, 80
Estimating materials, 25
Exotic wood species, 29

F

Fascia, installing, 164, 165
Fasteners, 38-39
  for decking, 110, 112, 117, 118-119, 121-123
  J-bolts, 39, 77-78
  for ledger attachment, 57, 58, 60
  replacing, 185
  threaded studs, 39, 80
Felt, roofing, use of, 37

Finish, applying, to deck, 180-181
Fir, Douglas, finishes on, 181
Flashing, 37, 55, 57, 58, 59, 60, 61
Floating-foundation decks, 37, 176-177
Floats and trowels, 83
    use of, 84
Footings, 68-85
    beam installation on, 97
    code regulations, 71, 81
    digging, 70-73
    estimating concrete for, 25
    fasteners in, 39, 77-78, 80
    inspection of depth, 24
    laying out, 62-65
    materials for, 37
    mixing concrete for, 74-75
    pads, concrete, 25, 82-85
    post bases, installing, 78-79
    pouring, 76-77
    precast concrete piers, 37, 81
Forms, concrete, for footings, 37
Framing, 86-87. *See also* Beams; Joists; Posts
    lumber for, 29
Framing connectors, 40
    for joists, 40, 99, 101, 103-104
    for posts, 40, 78-79
Freestanding benches, 166-168
Freestanding decks, 11, 18
    laying out, 18, 65, 67
Frost line and footings, 71
Furniture, seating, 10, 14, 34, 166-168

G
Glossary, deck, 8
Grades of lumber, 31
Ground-level decks, 17, 37
    beams, installing, 97
    forms for, 73
    on slab, 175
Ground-level pads, 83-85

H
Handrails, 36, 153-154
Hardware, 25, 87. *See also* Fasteners; Framing connectors
    with pressure-treated lumber, 28
Hatch, access, building, 115
Header joists, installing, 98, 102

diagonal, 101
double, 105
Heartwood vs. sapwood, 28, 29

I
Inspection of deck, 183-184
Inspectors, building, 24
Invisible fasteners, 39, 118–119, 121–123

J
J-bolts, 39, 77-78
Joints
    in rails, 146, 150, 152
    reinforcing hardware for, 40, 104
Joist hardware, 40, 99, 101, 103-104
Joists
    benches attached to, 168
    blocking, 103, 171
    cutting for curved deck, 173
    with diagonal beam, 17
    for floating-foundation deck, 177
    installing, 98-105
    matching synthetic decking, 33
    around obstructions, 104-105
    removing, 187
    spans, 20
    splicing, 104

L
Ladders, safety with, 51
Landings
    alternate materials for, 83
    building stairs with, 134-137
    ramp, 140
Laser level, use of, 45
Lattice
    privacy screen, 169
    railings with, 147
    roofs, 172
    skirting installation, 164-165
    windbreak, 11
Layout and marking tools, 41
    use of, 44-45
Layout of decks, 52-67
    footings, 62-65
    freestanding, 65, 67
    ledger installation, 54-61
    small decks, options for, 66

Ledger installations, 54-61
    for floating-foundation deck, 177
    long ledger, 61
    on masonry, 58-59
    materials for, 37
    for overhead structures, 172
    removing, 187
    on siding, 54-57
    on stucco, 60-61
Levels, 41
    use of, 44-45, 62
Lighting, low-voltage, 174
Load on deck, 21, 35
Lumber
    defects in, kinds of, 30
    estimating, 25
    finish choices for, 180, 181
    grades, 31
    preservative, treating with, 88
    sizes, 29, 31
    span calculations, 20-21
    storage, 31
    supporting, 51
    type, choosing, 28-29
    waste reduction, 23

M
Maintenance, deck, 178-179
    cleaning, 182-183
    inspecting, 183-184
Marking and measuring tools, 41, 42
    use of, 44-45
Masonry
    for landings, 83
    ledger installation on, 58-59
Masonry anchors, 39
Materials, choosing, 26. *See also* Lumber
    for concrete reinforcement, 82
    estimating needs, 25
    felt, flashing, and footings, 37
    hardware, 38-40
    railing components, 34, 36
    synthetic, 32-35
Measuring and marking tools, 41, 42
    use of, 44-45
Metal balusters, coated, installing, 156-158
Milled railing components, 36
Miter cuts

balusters with, 145
checking angle of, 49
with circular saw, 47
compound, 49, 155
marking, 45
mitersaws, use of, 49, 155
Multilevel decks, 9, 10, 16
box steps, 113

N

Nails, deck, 38, 112
replacing, 185
Nominal lumber sizes, 29
Notches, cutting
in decking, 113-114
in ledger, for vent, 61
in posts, 90-92

O

Obstacles, building around, 13, 104-105
notches for, 61, 113-114
Open stringers, 127, 133
making, 128-131
Overhead structures, 11, 13
building, 170-172

P

Pads, concrete, 82–85
estimating concrete for, 25
Paving for landings, 83
Pergolas, 11, 13, 170-172
Piers, precast concrete, 37, 81
floating-foundation decks with, 37, 176-177
Planning. *See* Design and planning considerations
Plans, drawing, 22-23
Planters, railing, 168
Plan view, 22
Post caps for railings, 36, 161
Posts
beam attachment to, 93-95
beam spans between, 21
bracing, 97, 177
for floating-foundation deck, 176
hardware for, 39, 40, 77-80
notching, 90-92
for overhead structure, 170, 171
plumbing, 45
privacy screen attached to, 169

railing. *See* Railing posts
setting and cutting, 88-89
sizing, 21
Power tools
augers, 70
basic selection, 43
circular saws, 46-48, 51
compound mitersaws, 49, 155
concrete mixers, 75
drills and drill bits, 43, 156
reciprocating saws, 50
washers, 183
Precast concrete piers, 37, 81
floating-foundation decks with, 37, 176-177
Pressure-treated (PT) lumber, 28, 29
freshly cut, treating, 88
Privacy screen, building, 169

R

Rafters for overhead structures, attaching, 171, 172
Railing posts, 36, 144-147
attaching, 149, 154
at corners, treatment of, 145
ganging for notching, 144
protruding, 144, 154
reinforcing, 147
for stair railings, 149-152, 154
for synthetic systems, 159, 161
through posts, 146
Railings, 10, 17, 24, 142-161
for angled stairs, 154-155
basic installation procedure, 148-154
components, 34, 36. *See also* Balusters; Railing posts
detail drawing, 23
estimating lumber for, 25
planters on, 168
removing, 187
synthetic, 34, 159-161
Rails, 36
attaching, 149
cap rails, 144, 152-153, 154, 158
with coated metal balusters, 156, 157, 158
corners, 145
joints in, 146, 150, 152
with lattice, 164, 169
planters on, 168
stair, 148-152, 153-155, 158

synthetic systems, 159-161
Raised decks, 9, 15
Raised pads, pouring, 85
Ramp, access, building, 139-141
Rebar, 77, 82
cutting, 84
Reciprocating saws, using, 50
Rental of tools, 27
Repairs, deck, 183, 185
Rim joists, installing, 98-99
Rip cuts, 47
marking, 45
Rise and run of steps, calculating, 127
Roofs, lattice, 172

S

Safety, 51
demolition of deck, 187
hole digging, 70
with pressure-treated lumber, 28
Sapwood vs. heartwood, 28, 29
Saw blades
circular, 48
reciprocating, 50
Saws, power, 43
circular, 46-48, 51
compound miter, 49, 155
reciprocating, 50
Scarf joints in rails, 146, 152
Schedule, making, 52-53
Screeding, 77, 84
Screen, lattice. *See* Lattice
Screws, 38, 39
for decking, 110, 117
for ledger attachment, 57, 58, 60
Scribe, framing, for curved deck, 173
Sealer, need for, testing, 181
Seating, 10, 14, 34
building, 166-168
Second-story access, decks with, 9, 15
Shade, providing for, 11, 12, 13
Siding, ledger installation on, 54-57
Site plans, 22-23
Site selection, 12-13
Size considerations for deck, 14
Sizes of lumber, 29, 31
Skirting, installing, 164-165
Slab, installing decking on, 175

Sleepers, installing, on slab, 175
Slopes, decks on, 9, 12
    footings for, 71
Soil as factor in site selection, 12
Span tables, 20-21
    for synthetic decking, 35
Spindles, railings with, 147
Splices for joists, 104
Sprayers, finish, 180
    use of, 181
Squaring, 44
    3-4-5 triangle for, 65
Stains, finishing with, 180, 181
Stairs, 10, 15, 124-138
    angled, 16, 154-155
    calculating measurements for, 126-127
    curved, synthetic, 35
    estimating lumber for, 25
    with landing, 83, 134-137
    for multilevel decks, 16, 113
    railing installation, 148-152, 153-155
    stringers. See Stringers
    wraparound, 138
Steps. See Stairs
Storage
    benches for, 10
    of lumber, 31
    behind skirting, 165

Stringers, 127
    closed, 127, 132-133
    diagonal, 138
    inspecting, 183, 184
    installing, 136–137
    open, 127, 128-131, 133
    ramp, installing, 140-141
    removing, 187
Stucco, ledger installation on, 60-61
Studs, threaded, 39, 80
Style and construction, 15-18
Synthetic materials, 32-35
    decking, installing, 116-120
    railings, 34, 159-161

T
Tape measures, 41
T-clips, synthetic decking installed with, 118-119
Tearing down of deck, 186-187
Thermoplastics, 32
3-4-5 triangle, 65
Through posts, 146
Toe-kick for stairs, 131, 137
Tools, 26-27. See also Power tools
    basic tool kit, 41-42
    for concrete work, 83, 84-85
    layout and marking, 41, 42, 44-45
    zip tool, 55

Track system, decking fastened with, 123
Tread installation
    ramp, 141
    stairs, 133, 136, 137
Trees, building around, 13, 104-105
Trowels and floats, 83
    use of, 84

V
Vents, notching ledger for, 61

W
Warped boards, 30
Waste reduction, 23
Water levels, use of, 44-45
Weather patterns, planning for, 11, 13
Wet-insert post bases, 79
Windbreak, lattice screen as, 11
Wood. See Lumber
Work site, setting up, 51
Wraparound decks, 10
Wraparound stairs, 138

Z
Zip tool, use of, 55

RESOURCES

eON Outdoor Living
151 Courtney Park Dr. W.
Mississauga, ON
L5W 1Y5
1-866-DIAL-EON
www.eonoutdoor.com

Trex Company, Inc.
160 Exeter Drive
Winchester, VA 22603
1-800-BUY-TREX
fax: 540-542-6880
www.trex.com
marketing@trext.com

UFP Ventures II, Inc.,
A Universal Forest Products Company
1801 E. Lessard, Prairie du Chien, WI 53821
877-462-8379
www.verandadeck.com

INDEX

Toolbox essentials: nuts-and-bolts books for do-it-yourself success.

Save money, get great results, and take the guesswork out of home improvement projects with a growing library of step-by-step books from the experts at The Home Depot.®

Packed with lots of projects and practical tips, these books help you design, remodel, decorate, and repair your home or garden. Easy-to-follow, step-by-step instructions and colorful photographs ensure success. Projects even estimate time, skills, materials needed, and tools required.

**You can do it.
We can help.**℠